THE
HISTORY
ATLAS OF
NORTH
AMERICA

The Macmillan Continental History Atlases

The History Atlas of Africa
The History Atlas of Asia
The History Atlas of Europe
The History Atlas of North America
The History Atlas of South America

THE
HISTORY
ATLAS OF
NORTH
AMERICA

Philip John Davies
David Ryan
David Brown
Ron Mendel
Foreword by Mark C. Carnes

MACMILLAN • USA

MACMILLAN

A Simon & Schuster Macmillan Company
1633 Broadway
New York, NY 10019-6785

Library of Congress Cataloging-in-Publication Data

Davies, Philip, 1948–
        The Macmillan history atlas of North America / Philip Davies;
(foreword by Mark C. Carnes).
                p.   cm.
        Includes bibliographical references and index.
        ISBN 0–02–862582–X
        1. North America—Historical geography—Maps.   I. Title.
II. Title: History atlas of North America   III. Title: Atlas of
North America.
G1106.S1 D3   1998   <G&M>
911'.7—DC21

                                                                                98–5401
                                                                                CIP
                                                                                MAPS

Manufactured in the United States of America
10 9 8 7 6 5 4 3 2 1

FOREWORD

No single geographical framework adequately encompasses the past. Over the past two centuries, the most common historical context has been the nation-state. Most professional historians specialize in the history of a single nation, and libraries and bookstores usually group history books by nation. Moreover, most secondary students throughout the world are obliged to study the history of their nation. All governments presume that the common grounding of a suitable history curriculum will promote sufficient national consciousness to ensure that young people become good citizens—or at least acquiescent taxpayers. The nation-state thus shapes our lives and has been a central force in modern history.

But the nation is not the only context for conceptualizing the past. Mountain ranges and inhospitable deserts have separated people far more effectively than political boundaries; on the other hand, some cultural forms, such as religions, languages, and popular culture, flow from one nation to another with astonishing ease. Though nations have attempted to control immigration, people often ignore national restrictions and irrepressibly seek opportunities wherever they can. Human activity and culture is not effectively bounded by the nation-state.

This atlas therefore undertakes a consideration of the entire continent of North America. One justification for this approach is that the main geographical features of the continent do not correspond to its national subdivisions, which mostly stretch east-west from the Atlantic Ocean to the Pacific. The Rocky Mountains cleave the continent along a north-south axis, defining a Pacific coastal rim that stretches from Alaska to the isthmus at Panama, leaving a vast plain in the center of the continent, drained by the Mississippi River and its tributaries; to the east lies the Atlantic coastal plain. Human settlement has often followed these natural paths. The earliest inhabitants, peoples from Siberia or northern China, crossed the land bridge at what is now the Bering Strait and trekked southward along either side of the Rockies; many thousands of years later, Spanish settlers and colonizers worked their way up the Pacific rim from Panama and Mexico to California; French colonists ranged along the St. Lawrence River and the Great Lakes and then paddled southward along the Mississippi to its mouth; English colonists, meanwhile, established footholds along the Atlantic coastal plain.

This historical atlas shows how war, political settlements, and economic and demographic forces eventually imposed national boundaries greatly at odds with the geography and historical precedents of the continent; the atlas also depicts the emergence of the United States as the dominant power on the continent.

The emergence in recent years of a global economy suggests, however, that even a regional orientation is insufficiently broad. Readers of this atlas may wish to consult the other volumes in this series to compare the developments in North America with those elsewhere in the world.

Mark C. Carnes
for the authors

CONTENTS

INTRODUCTION

For many people of North America there is a connection between on the one hand their sense of identity, and on the other, their sense of place. This holds true both for recent immigrants and for the native populations who predated them by thousands of years. Broad generalizations threaten to understate the complexity of communities among those who were the earliest population of the landmass, but time and again European observers, visitors, colonizers, invaders, and immigrants have been reminded that there existed in North America philosophies that owed nothing to the Old World. Visions existed of man as one of many respected inhabitants of a natural world that depended on symbiosis within the beneficence of the place where all lived together. These world structures were not without conflict—competition for resources was not a solely European practice—but there was an importance accorded to place in the early creation myths of the indigenous peoples of North America that continues to have influence in Native American communities.

For many of those entering the continent over the past 500 years the sense of place has been equally fundamental. Exploitation of real and imagined resources drove much early exploration, although many settlers had more complex reasons for moving to North America. By no means all migrants to North America were prompted by the need to escape oppression or religious or political persecution, or by lack of economic opportunity, but a significant proportion did feel these pressures. Their voices have colored the philosophies of the nations of North America. The United States of America, breaking itself by force from British colonial rule, did not wish to substitute any new form of continuous personalized political authority for the monarchical system that had been left behind. Canada, resisting various temptations to break away from Britain, has played a considerable part in educating the United Kingdom in the process of finding a role in a postcolonial world. The Commonwealth has provided a structure within which Canada has shown independent diplomatic skill and leadership, particularly on African issues. Canada continues to wrestle with the details of its constitutional balance, and worries about the cultural influence of its southern neighbor, but its responses to its population's ethnic mix, and to policy questions from health care provision to foreign affairs, are firmly stamped with an independently Canadian analysis and approach. Mexico has a separate legacy based on Spanish influence from Europe, with its Roman Catholic heritage, melded with the history and tradition of its indigenous peoples.

The indigenous population of North America showed a regional diversity that reflected the highly varying resources and challenges that faced dwellers in different parts of the continent. As the population of North America has grown and been added to, regional variation has continued to be a valued element of life. People define each other and others by region, as Southerners, Maritimers, Midwesterners, Oaxacans, and so on. These regional terms are more than simple categories. The geography of North America has continued to underpin varied lifestyles. The patterns of weather, soil, and minerals have been the foundation of various agricultures, industries, and economies in the regions of North America. The patterns of resource additions such as railways, highways, urban settlement, air routes, and educational institutions have developed and continued a rich pattern of regionally identifiable communities of interest.

These regional identifications have at times threatened the political unity of the nations of North America. The U.S. Civil War was the explosion of the most profound difference of opinion with a regional context. While the Union held, the differences subsequently did not go away. Tension emerged repeatedly between the forces of industry, finance, and banking in the East, and the farming and agricultural areas of the South and the West. While the U.S. Congress is today dominated by the two major political parties, members of Congress are very responsive to the regional needs of their home constituencies. Relatively loose party discipline among Democrats and Republicans allows U.S. senators and representatives the opportunity to press regional issues. A generation ago, a leading U.S. politician pointed out that all politics is local, and this continues to be a truism in U.S. politics. The Canadian West in its turn began to feel that the Ottawa-based government was less responsive to the concerns of distant regions than it should be. The addition of this tension to the long-standing cohabitation of Francophone and Anglophone Canadians has contributed to a mold-breaking regional realignment of Canadian political parties in national government. Mexican political developement has often taken the form of tension between the central power of the capital, and the needs of the peripheral regions. Agrarian revolt has played a major part in the foundation of contemporary Mexico, and continues to be an influence. Meanwhile Mexico City attracts migrants as the myth of Eldorado used to, often with equally disappointing results as this huge modern city proves incapable of dealing with the influx.

Local loyalties notwithstanding, however, a shared sense of place does unite the nations and peoples of North America. The national anthems and emotionally powerful patriotic songs of these countries speak of the continent's physical splendor, and of it as a beautiful place in which to be free and at liberty.

North America certainly does have a physical geography and natural history that can be breathtaking, but there are places that are not so grand, and for the most part people live in the not-so-grand places. The nations established in North America have learned from the errors of the trans-Atlantic nations, but they too have been the site of appalling injustice and oppression. The removal of indigenous groups from traditional lands started almost from the point of first contact. The internment of Japanese Americans in the United States during the Second World War showed that the ability to behave intolerantly had not disappeared centuries later. Nonetheless, however flawed in practice, there can be few places in the world where the rhetoric of political freedom and personal identity and the sense of place are so interwoven.

Philip Davies
for the authors

PART I: ENCOUNTERS AND REACTIONS

Christopher Columbus was not the first European to visit North America, nor did he ever accept that North America was where he had been. In spite of making four voyages across the Atlantic between 1492 and 1502, he persisted in the belief that he had traveled west as far as previously unknown outposts of Asia. Nonetheless, Columbus, the Admiral of the Ocean Sea, is credited with the initiation of contemporary, informed world interest in North America, and the whole span of North American time previous to his footfall on the Bahamian island of San Salvador is referred to as pre-Columbian.

A soapstone pipe, depicting a warrior beheading his victim. Smoking had religious overtones and elaborate pipes were created exclusively for ceremonial use.

Pre-Columbian North America was not a place of documents, and as such is one of the late prehistoric areas of the world. But prehistory is not the same as "without history." The peoples of North America lived in societies of hunters, gatherers, fishers, and farmers that contained and continued the experience and wisdom of previous generations. As sites have been examined, archaeologists have debated the probable size of the pre-Columbian North American native population. For many years, a population around fourteen million, concentrated largelely in and around the empire of the Aztecs, was accepted as accurate, but more recent works suggest a new figure of around fifty million. In either case, there has been discovered much evidence of a patchwork of thriving, trading, sometimes belligerent societies with complex religious beliefs and ritual, having developed over many thousands of years.

Relations between the peoples of the Old World and the New were complex. While they had a rhetorical commitment to treat the natives well, early explorers thought little of capturing a few natives to exhibit to their sponsors in Europe. Good relations were established in some cases, and ill-treatment of the native Americans was formally regretted, but perceived transgressions by the local populations were met with severe punishments. The Europeans remained anxious about the reliability of the indigenous groups, and some settlements did suffer from attack. Contact with Europeans coincided with a catastrophic decline in native populations, accelerated in large part by the importation of diseases to which the North American population had no immunity. Measles, smallpox, and typhus killed huge populations at speed. In the Caribbean island of Hispaniola, colonized by Columbus, the native population collapsed from half a million to a few hundred in the twenty-five years following the European arrival. Some Europeans felt this biological attack on the American Indians to be a welcome divine intervention.

Not all contacts were necessarily catastrophic. While the Europeans were learning of potatoes, maize, and tobacco, the Native Americans were gaining knowledge of horses and of different metals, thereby accelerating their technological development. But the Europeans were strong, they had the advanced weaponry, and they were driven by a desire for knowledge, power, and resources that was firmly founded on a sense of the moral rightness of their position.

The European Renaissance brought a new sense of conviction in political and cultural affairs. There was an increasingly prevalent shared belief in the improvements in quality of life brought by the development of trade. Merchant adventurers were ready to invest in high-risk exploration for the sake of commensurably high potential profits. The nations of Europe were looking for ways to enhance their power, authority, and economic strength, and monarchs were willing to sponsor overseas adventures, sometimes by actual investment, and in other cases by contracting to share the profits with entrepreneurs in return for royal patronage. In addition, the Roman church, a powerful political and motivational force, was eager to encourage the exportation of its religious beliefs and to expand its geographical reach.

Within months of Columbus's setting sail across the Atlantic, Pope Alexander VI published the papal bull *Inter cetera divina* and negotiated the Treaty of Tordesillas. These divided new discoveries to the west between the exploring Catholic nations of Spain and Portugal, and made the Spanish and Portuguese monarchies the agencies of the church in these new lands. Alexander was Rodrigo Borgia, father of the infamous Lucrezia and Cesare (the model for Machiavelli's political treatise *The Prince*). He was politically skilled, ambitious, cultured, and knowledgeable. He embodied the power that could be gathered by combining secular and religious authority with intrigue, bribery, patronage, and a ruthless focus on objective results. His intervention in the exploration of America minimized the risk, and potential costs, of rivalry between the Catholic seagoing nations, and added the inspiration of religious proselytization to the more secular stimuli for exploration.

The fifteenth-century invention of modern printing in Europe helped to disseminate knowledge, and to stimulate intellectual and commercial interest in new ideas, discoveries, and opportunities. The early market for the printed word was not a mass market, as costs were still high and education sufficient to read still a relatively rare commodity, but over time the public's skills improved, and the production of the printed word, and of printed illustration, became more commonplace and more widely accessible. Published documents played an important part in the definition and development of North America after the first European contact. The Spanish and Portuguese expeditions led by Vespucci appear to have explored the coasts of what are now Guyana, Brazil, and points to the south, but they led him to propose that this was not Asia, but was indeed a New World. In 1507, Martin Waldseemüller printed his own pamphlet commenting on these discoveries and proposing that the new lands be named, in honor of the explorer Amerigo Vespucci, America. Once in print, the name came into common use, and was later also applied to the northern part of the "New World."

News of discoveries was spread by the printed word; contracts for exploration and exploitation of land and articles of government, were documented; serious philosophies were written that took account of these discoveries; adventures were published that built on this accumulating knowledge. As publication became

The system of using "chinampas," or gardens on floating rafts, from a painting by Jose Muro Pico.

more common, so the impact of the New World on the ideas of the Old became more evident. As public debate about emergent issues developed, so the impact of the competing systems of thought became more open, though no less controversial. The fact that the European discovery of North America coincided with a period of expansionist thought and development in trade, religion, invention, and politics makes it fitting that North America should become the location for a nation-building exercise in which published ideas and information in pamphlets, books, maps, and broadsheets were to be all-important.

The adventure of exploration reached different populations in different ways. William Shakespeare, probably not an overseas traveler himself, nonetheless learned of other lands and other peoples, and put them, sometimes fancifully, into his works. Shakespeare was acquainted with the London-based backers of the Virginia colonies, and his final play, *The Tempest*, may have been influenced by his knowledge of their activities. Certainly the play's themes of contact between the learned Europe and the exotic, possibly magical new worlds, and of the European growing to maturity influenced by a new environment, were recognized by audiences. James I of England, a sponsor of colonial development, was especially interested in the play, commanding several private performances before the court at Whitehall.

European interpretations of North America included visions of the place as violent and terrible, as grand and awesome, as peopled by aggressive heathens, and as peopled by "noble savages." Certainly the early attempts at settlement were fraught with difficulty as migrants battled to survive in the face of unfamiliar conditions. Spanish settlement progressed slowly into the Southwest, but early English attempts failed repeatedly, and at the beginning of the seventeenth century there were no English settlers in North America. Thereafter migration gathered pace, and a critical mass was reached that could support trade, expansion, and community development. By the end of the seventeenth century, there were about 250,000 persons in the English colonies.

Not all migrants were willing. Slavery was well established in North America in the early years of European settlement; it continued as a legal system for over two hundred years, and underpins a racial heritage that lasts to this day. About 50,000 British convicts were transported in the eighteenth century, but however miserable their condition, these people, unlike slaves, at least enjoyed the prospect of eventual freedom. Also moved against their will were those indigenous peoples who increasingly found their land invaded by forceful European settlers.

North America in the mid-eighteenth century was not a land of utopian freedom. Religious communities that had fled the intolerance of England often proved intolerant, in their turn, of those who thought differently, and occasionally fell into hysterical recriminations. In 1637, Anne Hutchinson was driven from Providence, Rhode Island, for her challenges to the local religious authority, and such quarrels contributed to the development of new towns, settlements, and colonies as the population divided into camps. The expulsion of the Francophone Acadians from the Maritimes by the Anglophone authorities in the 1750s was an act of bitter ethnic intolerance.

These and other examples notwithstanding, North America was the site for new experiences in self-determination. Virginia elected its General Assembly in 1619, using a broader electorate than would ever have been considered in any European nation. The Mayflower Compact of 1620, a simple instrument of consensual government composed and signed by the Pilgrims who landed in Massachusetts, established a precedent for political development in the American colonies.

The very distance of North America from the European capitals meant that as its communities grew they had to be effectively self-governing and self-managing, at least in domestic matters, even while they were colonies of Europe. By the late 1700s, the various settlements in North America were poised to take different political paths, each of which would express in some part the maturity and individuality of the New World.

HUMAN MIGRATIONS

Among the diverse societies that developed in pre-Columbian America were the Tlingit people of the Northwest Coast. This carved and painted board shows ancestry and social position. These boards were attached to house posts and depicted different aspects of the family group's history.

Despite much recent interest in Native American culture and society, the origins of North America's indigenous peoples remain ambiguous. A number of theories have been put forward to explain the original peopling of North and South America, variously locating the migration from Europe, Africa, or Asia, and even suggesting that Native Americans were Ancient Egyptians, the lost tribe of Israel, or survivors from Atlantis. Such a lack of consensus reflects the difficulty historians face in uncovering evidence about native tribes, most of which have left no written records. This is particularly true of North American Indians, in contrast to the larger, more powerful civilizations of the Mayas, Aztecs, and Incas to the south. Indeed, the pre-Columbian period of North American history has largely been left to archaeologists and anthropologists working with fragmentary remains, ranging from small artifacts such as tools, pots, and weapons, to the more substantial earthworks and burial mounds.

However, one theory has commanded more support than others and stands as the most likely explanation of human migration to the region. Sometime during the last Ice Age, people from the eastern rim of Asia, present-day Siberia, moved across a temporary land bridge spanning the Bering Strait into the northwestern tip of the Americas. The formation of vast glaciers, covering thousands of miles, had caused the sea level to drop by as much as 300 feet, creating a grassy, tundralike terrain, called Beringia, which connected the two continents. It is estimated that passage was possible at various times between 70,000 and 30,000 years ago; between 25,000 and 15,000 years ago; and finally between 14,000 and 10,000 years ago. After that, the New World was cut off from the Old, save by sea travel, allowing for the unique development of each region.

From that point, small groups slowly traveled southward through Alaska along an ice-free corridor, into the northern plains of what is now known as the United States and Canada, and dispersed across the vast glacier-free expanses of North, Central, and South America. Archaeological remains prove that virtually the whole of the Americas was populated by 12,000 years ago, and other finds suggest human settlements from the Pacific to the Atlantic coast by as early as 35,000 years ago, a quite remarkable achievement considering the distances involved. This movement was a natural progression of human evolution, as small bands of hunter-gatherers followed their prey into uninhabited regions, to take advantage of the natural vegetation and wildlife and establish a permanent presence. Paleo-Indians, as these first inhabitants were called, lived in small groups and remained nomadic, although usually within well-defined boundaries. As the Earth's atmosphere warmed and the glaciers retreated, the landscape began to change into its present-day shape, which allowed for a more settled way of life. Between 8000 and 1500 BC, archaic Indians began to utilize the environment more effectively, hunting smaller mammals, fishing, and cultivating plants. Tribes generally became larger and more distinctive as they adapted to local conditions. By AD 1500, an incredibly diverse number of Indian societies, with distinct economies, languages, and cultures, were in place, as well as a complex system of trade networks, political affiliations, and religious practices.

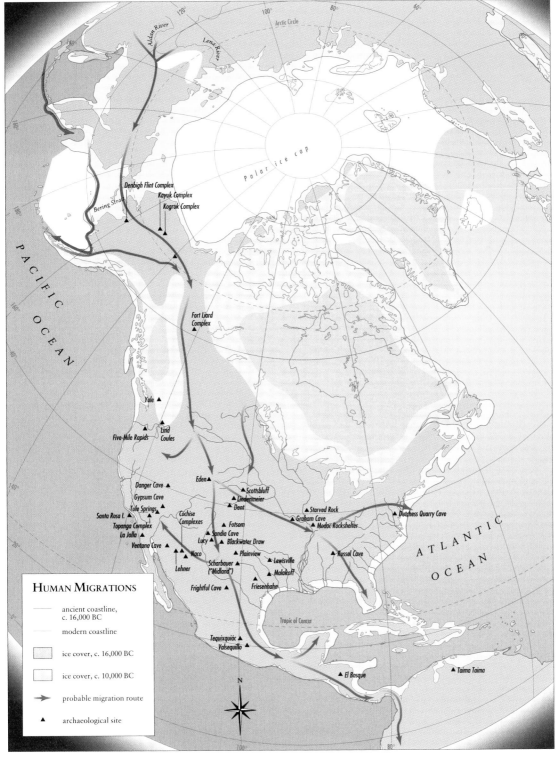

Denbigh Flint Complex
Kayuk Complex
Kogruk Complex

Bering Strait

Aldan River
Lena River
Arctic Circle

Polar ice cap

PACIFIC OCEAN

ATLANTIC OCEAN

Fort Liard Complex

Yale ▲

Lind Coules
Five-Mile Rapids ▲

Eden ▲
Scottsbluff ▲
Lindenmeier ▲
Dent ▲

Danger Cave ▲
Gypsum Cave ▲
Tule Springs ▲
Santa Rosa I. ▲
Topanga Complex
La Jolla ▲
Ventana Cave ▲

Cochise Complexes

Fotsom ▲
Sandia Cave ▲
Lucy ▲ Blackwater Draw
Naco ▲
Plainview ▲
Lehner
Scharbauer ("Midland") ▲
Frightful Cave ▲

Lewisville ▲
Malakoff ▲
Friesenhahn ▲

Starved Rock ▲
Graham Cave ▲
Modoc Rockshelter ▲

Russel Cave ▲

Dutchess Quarry Cave ▲

Tropic of Cancer

Tequixquiac ▲
Valsequillo ▲

El Bosque ▲

Taima Taima ▲

N

HUMAN MIGRATIONS

ancient coastline, c. 16,000 BC

modern coastline

ice cover, c. 16,000 BC

ice cover, c. 10,000 BC

→ probable migration route

▲ archaeological site

15

FIRST PEOPLES

A shell gorget depicting a flying shaman, with wings and talons of a bird of prey, holding a human head in one hand. Originating from the Mississippian Southern Cult, c. AD 1000

Approximately 600 autonomous native groups have been identified within North America by AD 1500, speaking more than 170 different languages, with an estimated total population at somewhere between fourteen and fifty million. These statistics begin to illustrate the incredible diversity and complexity presented by indigenous peoples and the problems inherent in trying to broadly summarize their distinguishing characteristics. Certainly European colonists had little idea of the richness and variety of Native American societies in North America, from the Aleut hunters along the shores of the Arctic Ocean to the great empires of the Maya and Aztecs of Mexico in the south.

North of the Rio Grande, tribal groupings can be divided by geographical region into six specific areas: The Eastern Woodland; the Plains tribes; Southwest tribes; West Coast Indians; Northwest tribes; and the less populated Arctic and Subarctic region. Based upon environmental conditions, these categories emphasize the importance of the land in shaping Native American cultures. Technology and religion developed in response to the unique features of each location. However, it would be a mistake to assume that each area was entirely self-contained; economic and social exchanges took place across the continent.

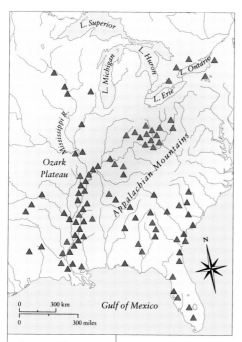

ADENA, HOPEWELL, AND MISSISSIPPIAN MOUNDS

▲ major Adena or Hopewell mounds, 1000 BC–AD 1000

▲ major Mississippian mounds, AD 700–1700

The Eastern Woodland stretched from the edge of the Great Lakes to the Gulf Coast, and from the Mississippi valley to the Atlantic Coast. It offered vast resources of abundant wildlife, fertile soil and vegetation, and forests essential for building. Along the Atlantic seaboard, tribes such as the Creek, Cherokee, Delaware, Iroquois, and Pequot occupied well-defined territories. They lived a seasonally sedentary lifestyle, based around hunting, gathering, and farming, and were organized into confederacies for political, military, and religious purposes. Farther to the west, the Mississippi valley had been the center of a great civilization, which was the first to achieve large-scale agricultural production on the rich alluvial floodplains of the Mississippi River. Although it had declined by the fifteenth century, the city of Cahokia once had a population of 20,000 people and controlled many neighboring tribes and villages.

The Great Plains, a vast expanse of grassland and shrub, was not so densely populated. Most tribes followed the millions of bison roaming the Plains, with only rudimentary cultivation. Plains Indians developed a highly mobile lifestyle, typified by the tepee, that remained unchanged for thousands of years. By the Missouri River, the Pawnee and Mandan lived a more sedentary existence based upon corn agriculture, more characteristic of the Eastern Woodland.

The Southwest was a dry, barren environment which posed testing problems for human habitation. Farming tribes such as the Hopi, Anasazi, and other Pueblo peoples developed irrigation systems and experimented with crop production, showing great ingenuity in taming the land. Living in small groups, they were architecturally advanced, building dwellings made of stone or adobe. Present-day New Mexico was once the site of a powerful confederation of twelve villages, centered in Chaco Canyon, that constructed a system of roads connecting satellite communities as far as sixty-five miles away. However, a severe drought in the thirteenth century curtailed expansion and dispersed the population back into smaller scattered groups.

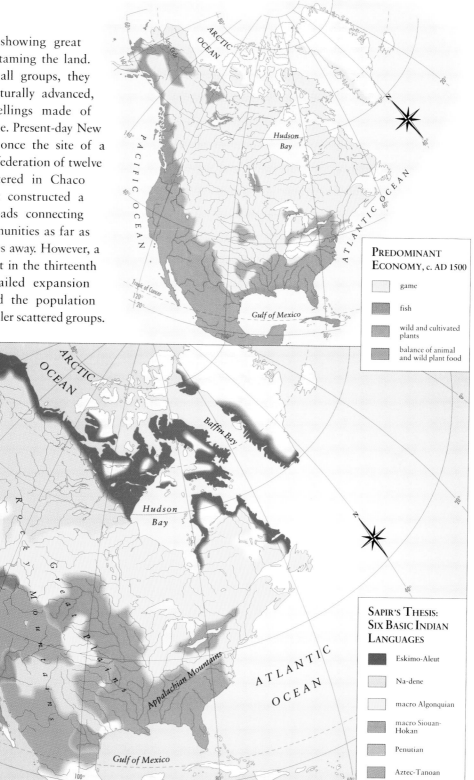

PREDOMINANT ECONOMY, c. AD 1500

- game
- fish
- wild and cultivated plants
- balance of animal and wild plant food

SAPIR'S THESIS: SIX BASIC INDIAN LANGUAGES

- Eskimo-Aleut
- Na-dene
- macro Algonquian
- macro Siouan-Hokan
- Penutian
- Aztec-Tanoan

CONTACT AND EUROPEAN EXPLORATION

"The Narragansett are the most beautiful people and have the most civil customs that we have found on this voyage . . . we made great friends with them."
Giovanni da Verrazano, extract from a letter to King Francis I of France, 1524

The Vikings extended the boundaries of European seafaring. In the late 900s, Erik the Red persuaded his followers to settle on Greenland, and further exploration to the shores of North America certainly took place. Evidence is limited, but the archaeological remains of one Norse settlement at L'Anse aux Meadows, in the north of Newfoundland, confirm the claims of the sagas that Norsemen reached America. The Norse made trading contacts with Inuit peoples, and may have met American Indians, but the resources of the Norse did not stretch to colonial development. The stories of these lands did spread, however, and the abundant fish and whales attracted ships from a number of European countries to the waters off North America.

The incentive to explore more thoroughly was provided by the growing significance of trade to the European economy. There was a drive for expansion in the fifteenth century, and the goods of the East, especially spices, were high-value commodities. Genoese-born sailor Christopher Columbus convinced the Spanish crown to sponsor a westward exploration. The world being round, he reasoned, this must mean a route to Asian riches, avoiding the difficult passage around the Cape of Good Hope that the more conventional voyage entailed.

Columbus made his landfall on an island in the Bahamas that he called San Salvador on October 12, 1492, and recorded his first meeting with the native peoples that he called Indians. Columbus, who made three further voyages to the region, always firmly believed that he had reached Asia.

Tales of the riches of the Americas added further stimuli for exploration, and various Spanish adventurers traveled to the islands and shores of the Caribbean. In 1513, Vasco Núñez de Balboa crossed the central American isthmus and saw the Pacific, but found no strait to Cathay. In 1519, Hernán Cortés began his conquest of the Aztecs, looting its wealth, feeding European visions of cities of gold in the New World.

Meanwhile John Cabot, also born in Genoa, but patronized by an English king, had, in 1497, traveled across the North Atlantic in search of a route to the Indies. He too failed, but recorded his visits to Newfoundland and the evidence of indigenous human presence. There were still hopes that a route to China would be found, but the options gradually diminished as other explorers filled in the unmapped sections of North America's Atlantic Coast.

Contacts with local peoples took various forms. The explorers were often welcomed, and simple trading took place. However, the native peoples often suffered at the hands of the newcomers. Gaspar Cortés Real captured and took away fifty-seven Beothuk Indians on a visit to Newfoundland. European diseases such as smallpox also invaded North America, sometimes destroying whole tribes of Native Americans. With more experience of Europeans, the local peoples became more wary. When Giovanni da Verrazano reached Casco Bay, Maine, in 1524, the native group made it clear by their shouts and gestures that he was not at all welcome. Contact with the existing North American peoples turned from trading to competition for land. Tensions and conflict were inevitable, and the technology of power was heavily biased in favor of the Europeans.

Daily life before the Spanish conquest: the market at Tlaxcala, a scene from a mural by Xochitiotzin.

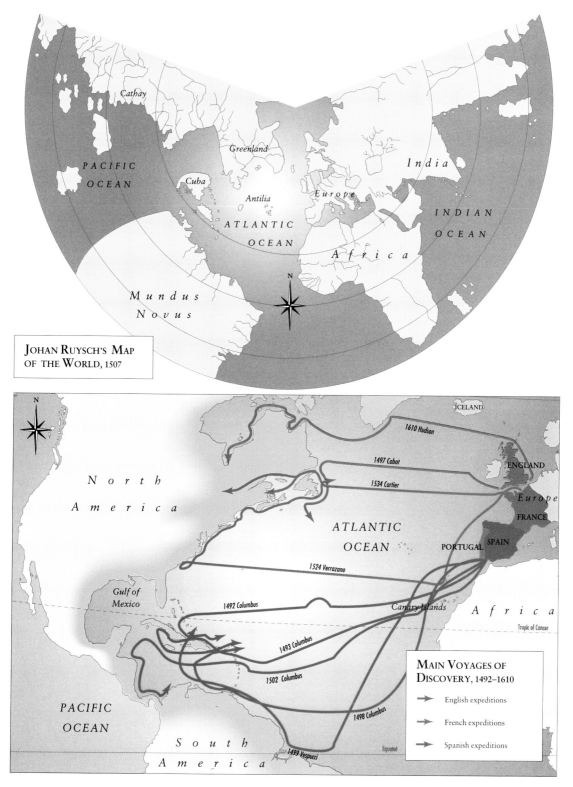

JOHAN RUYSCH'S MAP
OF THE WORLD, 1507

MAIN VOYAGES OF
DISCOVERY, 1492–1610

English expeditions

French expeditions

Spanish expeditions

NEW SPAIN, NEW FRANCE

England was not the only country looking toward North America. France and Spain had a significant presence and a great rivalry with England until at least the latter half of the eighteenth century.

Spanish presence was primarily an extension northward of the great empires acquired by conquering the Aztecs and Incas. Spain established the first permanent European settlement at St. Augustine, Florida, in 1565 as well as introducing the Catholic branch of the Christian faith to North America. Missionaries and explorers traveled across the southern rim of the present-day United States, which they called the Borderlands, the most important areas of Spanish occupation being Florida, California, and New Mexico. However, the northern edge of New Spain was never as important to the mother country's interests as the well-established and long-lasting control of Central and South America. Native Indian resistance and the failure to find comparable mineral wealth in the area undermined attempts at consolidation, as illustrated by events in New Mexico. In 1598, Juan de Oñate led an expedition to present-day New Mexico. When a native village refused to hand over water and food, the invaders killed 800 Indians and treated the survivors brutally. Other Pueblo Indian villages acquiesced to Spanish rule, formalized by the founding of Santa Fe in 1610. However, when no gold was found, most Spaniards left the area, leaving behind a handful of government officials and Christian missionaries. Over the next seventy years, Franciscan friars worked conscientiously to convert the natives, who refused to abandon tribal beliefs. In 1680, tired of Spanish interference, the native peoples conducted the Pueblo Revolt, which killed 400 colonists and drove the Spanish out of New Mexico for twelve years. This culmination of many years of opposition was the most successful and sustained indigenous resistance movement in colonial North America. Although Spain restored authority in 1692, it was upon the basis of cooperation, not coercion.

A map of colonial Boston and Charlestown, showing the fortifications dating from about 1776.

Thus, Spanish outposts in North America were primarily maintained for strategic and religious purposes. Fearful of the encroachment of France and England on the Atlantic Coast, and Russian and English designs on the Pacific Coast, Spain supported a number of thinly populated forts and missions across the Borderlands in the hope of keeping out her rivals.

French interests concentrated upon the area far to the north. Following the pioneering exploration of Jacques Cartier in the 1530s, Samuel de Champlain founded Quebec in 1608. When Montréal was established in 1642, French control of the St. Lawrence valley was confirmed. The success of New France was primarily built upon the highly profitable fur trade, in partnership with local Indian tribes. In 1663, the charter of the private New France Company was revoked and replaced by royal direction in an attempt to stimulate low numbers of new arrivals. This policy had only limited impact and the population remained largely composed of hunters, traders, and Jesuit missionaries, but a small number of immigrants did set up farms on the St. Lawrence River between Montréal and Québec. By 1672, New France had a population of over 5,000 and although not as large as English colonies, had made a lasting impact on the region. The French were also the first Europeans to venture into the heart of the continent.

Although France and Spain claimed vast tracts of territory and might have appeared to be in a strong position, the demographic reality was quite different. By 1700, New France had 15,000 inhabitants, New Spain just 4,500, and the English colonies 250,000. The failure to attract large-scale immigration left French and Spanish settlements isolated and vulnerable.

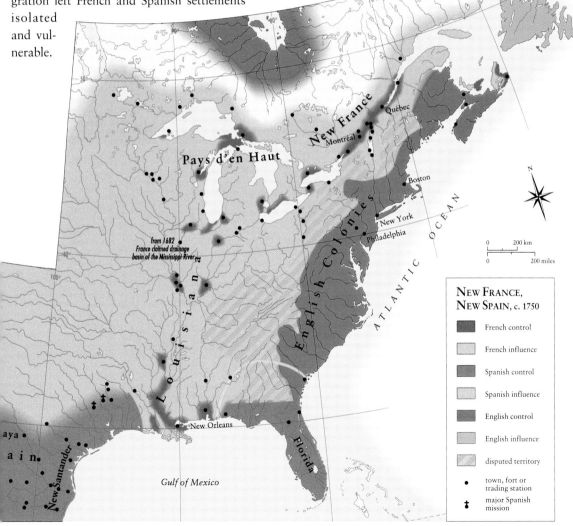

New France, Québec, Montréal

Pays d'en Haut

Boston

New York

Philadelphia

from 1682
France claimed drainage
basin of the Mississippi River

Louisiana

English Colonies

ATLANTIC OCEAN

0   200 km

0   200 miles

NEW FRANCE,
NEW SPAIN, c. 1750

French control

French influence

Spanish control

Spanish influence

English control

English influence

disputed territory

● town, fort or
trading station

✝ major Spanish
mission

aya ●

a i n.

New Santander

New Orleans

Florida

Gulf of Mexico

English Settlement: Virginia

Departure of the Puritans from Delft harbor to join the Mayflower. *A detail from a painting by Adam van Breen, 1620.*

The first permanent English settlement in North America was Jamestown, founded in 1607. Situated along the James River, the Virginia colony, named after Elizabeth I, "the Virgin Queen," grew in importance during the seventeenth century, as settlers spread out through the Tidewater region of the Chesapeake Bay.

In 1606, James I granted a charter to two groups interested in exploiting potential resources on the North American coast. The London Company and the Plymouth Company, a diverse mixture of merchants, aristocrats, and philanthropists, each sent an expedition the following year, one landing in Maine, the other in Virginia. The plan was simply to establish trading posts to collect furs, fish, timber, and other natural resources as well as to search for precious metals. Both expeditions found even this modest enterprise difficult to sustain, and the Plymouth Company was forced to withdraw from Maine. For a decade, the settlement in Virginia struggled on the brink of disaster. Initially, 104 men and boys arrived in the *Chesapeake* on May 6, 1607. They were joined by small numbers of others in the next two years, who were mostly motivated by a common desire to find immediate riches. Jamestown was situated adjacent to a mosquito-infested swamp that spread malaria and other diseases to the settlers, who were already having to cope with a severe shortage of food. As a consequence, the population went from 500 to sixty during the winter of 1609–1610, morbidly referred to as the "starving time." That the colony survived at all was largely due to the autocratic leadership of John Smith and later Thomas Dale.

In order to make Virginia more attractive to potential immigrants, drastic changes were made. Settlers were offered stocks in the London Company and more personal autonomy once in the colony. In 1618, the "headright" system granted fifty acres to paying new arrivals and the same amount of land to those who financed the passage of other laborers. Governor Francis Wyatt devoted substantial men and materials in

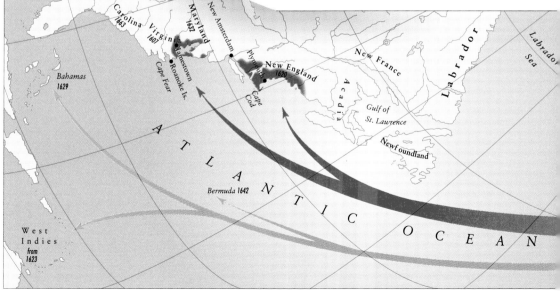

a bloody war of attrition against the Powhatan Indians. In 1624, James I revoked the company charter and reorganized Virginia as a royal colony.

The net effect of these developments was to bring some measure of stability to the colony. Left largely to govern its own affairs, Virginia progressed rapidly. Tobacco secured the economic success of the colony and helped to shape its character. The headright system encouraged the development of large plantations, and Virginia's ruling elite became dominated by powerful planters such as the Byrds, Carters, and Randolphs. Abundant land was offset by an acute shortage of labor, and the family dynasties created by the end of the seventeenth century were built on the hard work of others. Indentured servants repaid the cost of travel by working for a fixed term of between four to seven years and were by far the majority of Virginia's population. Despite greater opportunities in the New World than in Great Britain, indentured servants were not happy with their exploitation, and in 1676, Bacon's Rebellion forcibly signaled their collective discontent. Once order was restored, Virginia looked toward slavery to satisfy its labor requirements.

In contrast to Virginia, New England was founded upon idealistic notions that tried to create a utopian society. Puritans, English followers of John Calvin, rejected the "corrupt" nature of Catholicism and the Church of England and developed their own religion, based upon predestination, which condemned alcohol, gambling, and many aspects of English popular life.

The first group of Puritans arrived in the New World via Holland, where they had fled to escape persecution. Setting sail on the *Mayflower* on September 16, 1620, they made up only one-third of the ship's 102 passengers but effectively led the expedition. On November 9, they reached Cape Cod. After perusing the most advantageous point at which to disembark, the settlers decided upon Plymouth, which had first been discovered by John Smith, and landed on December 16, 1620.

> "Being thus arrived in a good harbor, and brought safe to land, they fell upon their knees and blessed the God of Heaven."
> *William Bradford*, extract from *Of Plymouth Plantation*

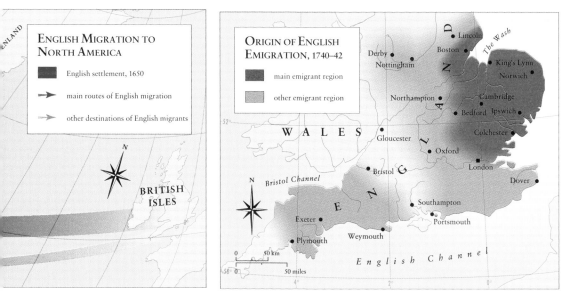

New Plymouth initially faced similar problems to Virginia's, and relied heavily upon the support of local tribes for their continued survival. Their eventual success inspired others to follow them and establish the ideal of a self-reliant, god-fearing folk, making a new beginning in a "promised" land.

These separatists were, however, overshadowed in importance by a different group of Puritans—the Congregationalists. Stimulated by the religious persecution that accompanied the succession to the throne of Charles I in 1625, Congregationalists did not want to split completely from the Church of England but to reform from within. America might offer the best location in which to do so. In 1629, a group of Congregationalist merchants obtained a royal charter granting permission to land on the East Coast, calling themselves the Massachusetts Bay Company. With John Winthrop elected as governor, the company decided to relocate its headquarters to New England. A year later, a group of 700 men, women, and children joined the initial party of 400 in Massachusetts. Winthrop's famous sermon on board the ship *Arabella* established the expectations for the new colony. He emphasized the communal nature of the project, urging personal desires to be secondary to the greater good of the congregation, and set out the model of a Christian lifestyle based upon charity and friendship. Winthrop's covenant was a collective agreement among the new arrivals to live up to God's expectations of a chosen people. These ideals proved difficult to put into practice but retained a powerful grip on the culture of the region, and wider American society, long after the 1630s.

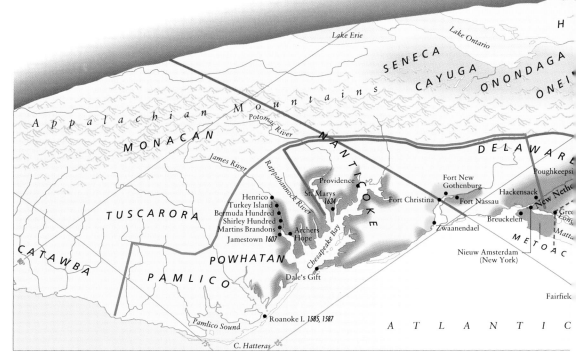

Approximately 22,000 immigrants arrived in the following decade, a movement known as the "great migration." Six settlements were established in the Massachusetts Bay in 1630, including Boston, and other towns and villages followed rapidly. This development proceeded in an egalitarian fashion, in the sense that new communities were granted considerable autonomy. Towns formed the basic political and administrative unit, and town leaders had the right to distribute land as they saw fit. Each community was required to build meeting houses, pay ministers' salaries, and, in 1634, send two delegates to the General Court. Puritans saw the basis of society as the family rather than the individual. Families were usually granted one acre of land no more than half a mile from the meeting house and could count on considerable support in times of emotional or economic distress. In general, New England was characterized by a high degree of social cohesion.

Nevertheless, religious and commercial tensions were apparent as well. Disagreements over scriptural interpretation led to the banishment of Anne Hutchinson, whose followers created New Hampshire in 1638, and the founding of Rhode Island in 1644 by Roger Williams. Numbers of colonists did not share the ideals of the Puritans. The need for fresh land saw the establishment of Connecticut in 1639. Farmers and merchants were more interested in profits than Scripture, and a number of bustling commercial towns developed around key transportation routes, seaports, and river terminuses. A conflict between idealism and materialism was apparent from New England's very founding.

EUROPEAN SETTLEMENT ALONG THE ATLANTIC COAST, c. 1660

HURON	Indian tribe
	British settlement
	Dutch settlement
	Swedish settlement
1634	date of settlement
◯	grant to Virginia Company of London
◯	grant to Virginia Company of Plymouth
◯	grant to Council for New England
- - -	Treaty of Hartford boundary between English and Dutch, 1650

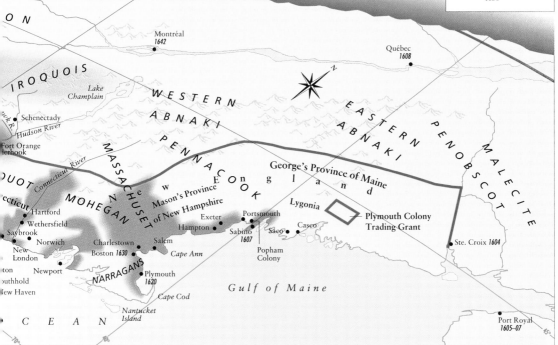

INDIAN/EUROPEAN RELATIONS

Relations between Europeans and the indigenous peoples of North America were marked by three distinct stages. First, there was an incredible exchange of plant and animal life between the Old and New Worlds, as centuries of geographical isolation came to an end. Crops taken for granted nowadays, such as potatoes, beans, squash, and maize, had such a nutritional impact upon the European diet as to fuel a population explosion. Europeans introduced wheat, rice, bananas, sugar, and wine grapes, which were quickly established across the Americas and became major exports back to Europe. Colonizers brought with them domesticated animals such as horses, cattle, pigs, sheep, and fowl, all previously unknown to Native Americans. These animals had a significant impact upon tribal lifestyles, as they were utilized for transport and clothing, as well as for food, but grazing animals were also responsible for destroying large acres of cropland. However, unquestionably the most devastating aspect of what has been termed "the Columbian Exchange" was disease. Native people had little immunity to European disease. Measles, influenza, diphtheria, tuberculosis, smallpox, and even the common cold decimated the New World as epidemics swept across the Americas. It was disease that was the major agent of European conquest, claiming far more lives than warfare. In turn, Indians passed on syphilis to Europeans, the first case being diagnosed in Barcelona in 1493.

The second stage involved trade and cultural interchange, as settlers lived side by side with Native Americans. Unfamiliar with local conditions and almost uniformly unprepared, the first colonists relied upon the help of local tribes for their survival. In New England, the Puritans were indebted to the Indian Squanto, who showed them how to fertilize the land and plant corn, an event celebrated by Thanksgiving today. In Virginia, relations with the powerful Powhatan Confederacy determined the success of the colony. It is unlikely that Pocahontas saved John Smith in the dramatic fashion portrayed by Hollywood, but she was an important diplomatic mediator between the English and Indians. Trade involved a range of goods. Europeans exchanged tools, beads, clothes, cloth, blankets, guns, and alcohol in return for Native expertise, land, and, most important, hunting skills. Animal pelts fetched a high price on European markets, and some Indian tribes fundamentally reoriented their activity in order to satisfy European demand. As game was exhausted, the natural ecological balance became disrupted, with far-reaching consequences for traditional ways of living. Missionaries brought Christianity to Indians, but captive Europeans, or "White Indians" taken in battle, often converted to Native ways more successfully.

The final phase of Indian-European contact was marked by increased friction and warfare. Once colonies had stabilized their position and attracted larger numbers of immigrants, the pressure to expand became irresistible. Derogatory myths of the Indian savage justified the colonists' actions as the strategic outlook went from the defensive to a more aggressive, expansionist policy. John Smith's response to the Virginia massacre of 1622, a desperate attempt by Indians to drive settlers off their land, indicated the deteriorating nature of the relationship—"now we have just cause to destroy them by all means possible." The major conflicts of the seventeenth century took place in New England. Puritans exploited long-standing rivalries between tribes to further their aims. In 1636–1637, the Pequots were wiped out by a combined force of colonists and Narragansett Indians. King Philip's War, 1675–1676, a bloody campaign waged over fourteen months, reduced southern New England's Indian population by 40 percent, and effectively signaled the end of Indian resistance in the area. Thus, a pattern was established that was repeated as English settlers moved west. It was not inevitable, as French settlers in Canada remained

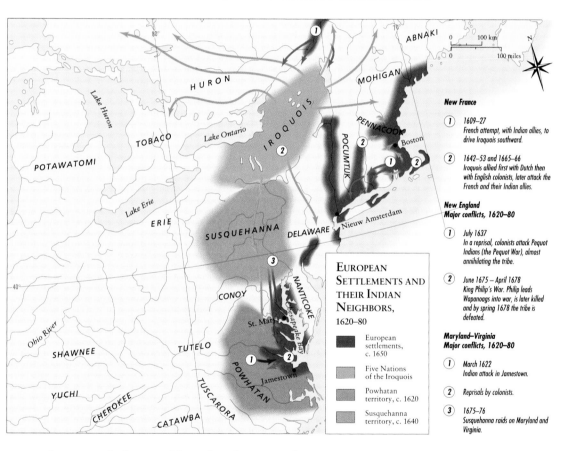

EUROPEAN SETTLEMENTS AND THEIR INDIAN NEIGHBORS, 1620–80

- ■ European settlements, c. 1650
- Five Nations of the Iroquois
- Powhatan territory, c. 1620
- Susquehanna territory, c. 1640

New France

1 1609–27
French attempt, with Indian allies, to drive Iroquois southward.

2 1642–53 and 1665–66
Iroquois allied first with Dutch then with English colonists, later attack the French and their Indian allies.

New England
Major conflicts, 1620–80

1 July 1637
In a reprisal, colonists attack Pequot Indians (the Pequot War), almost annihilating the tribe.

2 June 1675 – April 1678
King Philip's War. Philip leads Wapanoags into war, is later killed and by spring 1678 the tribe is defeated.

Maryland–Virginia
Major conflicts, 1620–80

1 March 1622
Indian attack in Jamestown.

2 Reprisals by colonists.

3 1675–76
Susquehanna raids on Maryland and Virginia.

on good terms with their neighbors, but that was reflective of the small numbers populating New France. In the English colonies, expansion was accomplished by increased numbers of settlers, their superior military capabilities, and the disunity of Indian tribes.

European subjugation of the Indians was not a uniform process but entailed varying interactions with different tribal groups. For example, the Iroquois, a confederation of five tribes based in upstate New York, were not significantly threatened by colonists for many years and held the balance of power between competing colonial powers. Only with the withdrawal of the French in 1763 was their position weakened.

THE SLAVE TRADE

"I should choose to be insured, and whatever Expence came to my Share more than slaves sent, I would remit by return of the vessel that bro't the slaves.
The whole voyage I leave to you to conduct and you may begin to prepare if you please."
Carter Braxton, from a letter sent to Nicholas Brown and Company of Providence, Rhode Island

Slavery had been a prominent feature of human society since ancient times, but the Atlantic slave trade was by far the largest, most sustained, and most highly organized forced movement of people into bondage. Its far-reaching impact cannot be overstressed, as the demographic shape of the globe was transformed.

Between the fifteenth and nineteenth centuries, an estimated twelve million Africans were forcibly taken from their homelands. Initially, the trade centered upon European markets, but when the New World was opened up for colonization, an insatiable need for labor created massive demand for African slaves. Approximately ten million Africans were sold in the New World, mostly in South America and the Caribbean (the rest either died in transit or were sold in Europe).

Britain gained control of the international slave trade in the seventeenth century, and cities like Liverpool and Bristol grew rich upon the profits. In general, those taken originated from West Africa, although traders looked southward and into the interior regions as demand exceeded supply. Slavery had been a long-standing feature of Africa, but under European direction it became more incessant and business-oriented. In exchange for European merchandise, such as weapons, alcohol, and manufactured goods, partnerships were established with African suppliers and forts were built on the West Coast to facilitate transportation. Nevertheless, it must be stressed that the trade was increasingly based upon coercion and irreparably damaged the development of some African societies.

Slaves came from a variety of backgrounds, but the majority were prisoners of war, criminals, or debtors. After capture, they faced the ordeal of the journey to the New World and their eventual sale. Known as the Middle Passage, the 6,000-mile voyage was hazardous in the extreme, and ships lost between 5 and 20 percent of their crew and human cargo.

In comparison to other New World slave societies, like the Spanish and Portuguese possessions, the United States received far fewer imports. Six hundred thousand American slaves amounted to just 6 percent of the total trade. The first Africans arrived in Virginia in 1619, but most passed through the major seaport of Newport, Rhode Island, before being sold on southern slave markets. In a society where most people were unfree laborers (indentured servants) of some kind, it is uncertain as to the status of those first arrivals. The legal status of slaves gradually evolved in the seventeenth and eighteenth centuries, with major slave codes passed in Virginia in 1680 and 1705, and in South Carolina in 1690, 1696, 1712, and 1740. These codes developed in response to increased arrivals and the need to maintain control. The vast majority of North American slaves came after 1700. In 1808, the international slave trade was banned in the United States, although this merely stimulated a flourishing internal trade and some illegal imports.

Fundamentally driven by economic imperatives, slavery made an indelible mark on North American society. Slaves made a critical contribution to the success of the colonies, although there were notable regional variations in their use and importance. In the North, where agriculture was generally small scale, slaves engaged in a variety of occupations but composed only a small proportion of the population. To the South, however, slavery became the basis of economic productivity. The upper South (Virginia, Maryland, and North Carolina) contained the largest number of slaves up to the Revolution, and tobacco production could not have been conducted on such a scale without their labor. As the soil became exhausted from 1750, planters turned their attention to other crops like wheat, but maintained the institution of slavery, which had become deeply ingrained in the economic and social fabric of the region. Although not as numerous until after 1800, slaves made up a greater proportion of the population of the lower South (South Carolina and Georgia). Rice was as central here as tobacco was in the Chesapeake, and it highlighted the skills of the African slaves; Europeans had only limited experience in growing rice.

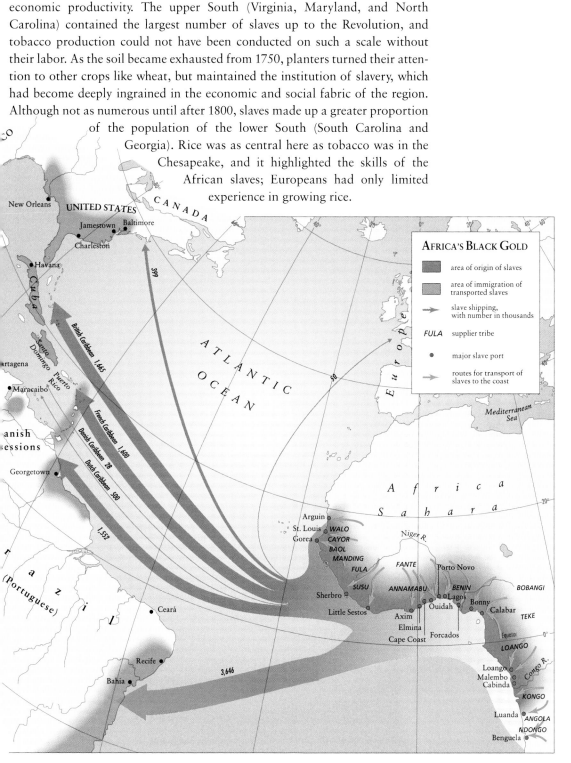

THE ATLANTIC COLONIES BY 1750

In the eighteenth century, mainland British North America largely consisted of scattered settlements in New England and the Chesapeake. However, by 1750, viable colonies from Massachussetts to Georgia had developed. Indicative of this metamorphosis was the exponential growth in the colonies' population. By midcentury, the population stood at 1.5 million, four times as great as it was at the beginning of the century.

High birthrates and a steady influx of immigrants accounted for this growth. Certain factors encouraged men and women to marry soon after reaching adulthood. A man without a wife would find running a farm or a store extremely difficult, and a young woman, with few opportunities to earn a livelihood and considered more an economic liability than an asset to her parents, found it desirable to seek a partner. Early marriages resulted in large families; on average a family had eight children and more than forty grandchildren. Between 1710 and 1750 alone, 350,000 Europeans migrated to the colonies; about half of them were German, Scots-Irish from Ulster, and Irish. Consequently, 80 percent of the population in 1700 was English or Welsh; by 1750, only 50 percent was.

Immigration was particularly important in the development of "newer" colonies. The Carolinas attracted Scots-Irish and Scottish settlers, especially beyond the tidewater areas. Pennsylvania, founded under the proprietorship of William Penn and other influential Quakers, became the home of German and Scots-Irish immigrant farmers, who continually redefined the frontier line of expansion. Among the German immigrants were members of small religious sects—the Dunkards, Amish, Mennonites, and Moravians. Other colonies possessed an equally diversified population. Swedish, Danish, and Dutch settlers joined English Anglicans and Quakers, Dutch Calvanists, and Scottish Presbyterians in New Jersey. New York's mixture of peoples resulted in the formation of a fractious colony where conflict boiled over in local elections and land riots by largely German and Dutch tenant farmers against their Anglo-American landlords.

By 1750, the Middle Atlantic colonies of New York, New Jersey, and Pennsylvania were challenging the preeminent position of Massachusetts and Virginia. In New York a colonial aristocracy had emerged, consisting of grandee landowners and wealthy merchants, whose power rivaled that of Virginia's planter elite. New York City and Philadelphia joined Boston as mercantile and economic centers. Pennsylvania's farmers, taking advantage of rich alluvial soil, grew wheat and corn and raised livestock for distant markets. Since the price of wheat tended to rise against the price of imported manufactured goods, the turn to commercial agriculture accelerated in Pennsylvania, in contrast to New England, where farming catering to the needs of the household prevailed. In any event, much of colonial

ECONOMY

- cattle and grain
- tobacco
- rice and indigo
- furs and skins
- fishing banks
- fishing
- lumber and timber
- shipbuilding
- ironworks

PREDOMINANT IMMIGRANT GROUPS, c. 1750

- English
- Scots-Irish
- Highland Scots
- Dutch
- French
- German
- Africans
- ✡ Jews
- ☐ Swedes
- △ Welsh
- ◇ French Huguenots

economic activity became increasingly integrated into a trading system that linked the British mainland colonies with Great Britain, Europe, the Caribbean, and Africa. Fish, lumber, flour, and live-stock left Boston, New York, and Philadelphia for the West Indies, which in turn supplied the mainland population with molasses and slave labor. The colonial seaports also exported furs, fish, naval stores, rice, and indigo to England, and furnished western Europe with meat, rum, and grain.

The earnings from these exports provided the American colonies an array of consumer goods. The urban homes of wholesale merchants and financiers, as well as those of the tidewater planta-tion owners, displayed their prosperity, with pur-chases of ornamental furniture, the latest fashions, and expensive cutlery and china. Notwithstanding that an export-led economy in the seaport cities left merchants and artisans vulnerable to volatile markets, easily disrupted by poor weather and war, the growth in trade proved to be a boon for colonial economic development.

To some observers this economic vigor represented another dimension of an environment and ethos that created a "new man," no longer servile but independent; no longer lacking in industry but driven by ambition; and no longer dull but intelligent. Others went even further, projecting the American colonies as the epi-center of the English speaking/thinking world, the last retreat of arts, imperial liberty, and truth. Such views in 1750 would resonate, with a slightly different meaning twenty-five years later, when a critical mass of Americans felt the time had come for the colonies to seek their independence from British rule.

PART II: NEW NATIONS

The leaders of North America in the second half of the eighteenth century had a range of intellectual and practical experience that would prove valuable to nation-builders. They had the practical experience of decades of working with some autonomy within the framework of a political authority that was thousands of miles distant. The colonies needed to be managed locally on a day-to-day basis, and this had led to the development of a political class throughout British North America. The settlement, exploration, and management of North America was effectively contracted out to companies and to emerging local governments. All of this was underpinned by documents and contracts outlining the obligations, responsibilities, and rights of those involved. Within the parameters thus established there had been the freedom to experiment at least in a limited way with articles of government, and with forms of representation.

The great written works of the age, including those of political thinkers such as Montesquieu and John Locke, traveled across the Atlantic to be read and discussed. Many learned through their reading and debate; some elite children were sent to be educated in Europe. Higher education in North America was small scale and generally motivated by the need to train a literate church ministry, but colleges were established at an early date, so not everyone desirous of a higher education needed to return to Europe for it. Harvard was founded in 1636, and with Yale (1701), the University of Pennsylvania (Philadelphia Academy, 1740), Princeton (Presbyterian College of New Jersey, 1746), Columbia (King's College, 1754), Brown (College of Rhode Island, 1764), and

The Declaration of Independence submitted to Congress, July 2, 1776. In this painting by Trumbell, Thomas Jefferson, surrounded by other members of the committee, is placing the draft of the Declaration on the table in front of Hancock.

Dartmouth (1769), most of what is now the Ivy League was established before the end of the 1760s. The College of William and Mary (1692) and Rutgers (1766) were also among these early foundations. In Canada the development of higher education progressed a little more slowly, but with such institutions as King's College, Halifax (1789), Dalhousie University (1818), McGill University (1821), and the University of Toronto (1827), the pattern was set for high quality. This early enthusiasm for university and college education indicated the value placed on learning and knowledge, and the tradition of public and private investment in higher education that continues to be a feature of life in North America.

The populations of what were to become the United States of America and Canada took different routes to nationhood in the second half of the eighteenth century. The political leaders who initiated these choices were well aware of the value of consensual government based firmly on agreed documents. They were versed in the historical, philosophical, economic, and political debates of the time, and were aware that choices were available to be made. They had come from communities that valued the resources of knowledge and education. They knew from experience that practical skills were also invaluable in developing economies and polities. They were able to draw on those elements of European society that were useful to them, while exercising the liberty of developing new approaches suitable to North America. There was no other place in the world where such a large society of recent migrants was establishing itself. Neither "rebels" nor "loyalists" were unthinking, but made their choices against the background of their experience in North America. The decision in the thirteen colonies was to fight for liberation from the colonial rule, while in Canada it was to remain linked to the home country.

The American War of Independence sharpened the ideas in the political debate. In the newly independent United States the form of government was set on a path toward being more inclusive. In Canada an elitist system emerged firmly in place. The Canadian colonial-aristocratic style could not remain inflexible. While it took some shocks to the system to stimulate a radical reevaluation, the country was engaged constantly by the need to respond to its bilingual European population, as well as to the demands of those Canadians who desired keenly never to be part of the United States, but pressed energetically for a broader-based, locally controlled political structure in their chosen country. The United States also was limited by the ideas of the times. The Constitution failed to recognize the rights of women, allowed black slavery to continue, and turned out to be of little practical support to the American Indian population. The debates on these issues continued for many years.

The people of the United States lacked a clear understanding of the land to the west. Spanish missions had been established in the Southwest and on the California coast throughout the seventeenth century. European settlement of these areas was generally slow, and native resistance had at times been fierce, but ultimately futile—the Pueblo rebellions of 1680 effectively expelled the Spanish

"When in the course of human events, it becomes necessary for one people to dissolve the political bonds which have connected them with another, and to assume among the powers of the earth—the separate and equal station to which the laws of nature and of Nature's God entitle them, a decent respect to the opinions of mankind requires that they should declare the causes which impel them to separation."
Thomas Jefferson, preamble to the Declaration of Independence, July 4, 1776

from New Mexico for more than a decade. Individual hunters and trappers traveled into relatively unknown territory, but the combined knowledge from all these sources did not produce an accurate description of the West.

It was recognized in the United States that the West could provide natural resources to stimulate trade, manufacture, and invention. Its lands could be a source of government revenue. The settlements that might move onto those lands would increase the reach of the nation, and the settlers would have a personal investment in the stability of that nation's political order. By passage of the Northwest Ordinance (1787), the United States enabled the simple establishment of new, politically recognized territories, and ultimately states, under the wing of the United States. A later administration seized the opportunity to expand the nation's territorial claims by the purchase from France of the Louisiana Territory. Since the French did not have a very accurate idea of what they were entitled to sell, the Americans needed to define their claim quickly and authoritatively. Meriwether Lewis and William Clark were dispatched by President Jefferson to explore and to report back. Two years of exploration produced maps

A Shoshoni hide painting depicting a buffalo dance after a successful hunt. The mounted figure wears a war costume. His long feather trailer indicates his status.

and descriptions that added significantly to available knowledge, and stimulated further mobility. Jefferson prompted further government encouragement by commissioning a survey for a national road to ease the trek into the nation's heartland. Construction of the National Road began in 1811, and reached the middle of Illinois by 1838.

America's population was growing. In 1790, the first U.S. census counted 3.9 million persons. The national population was to grow by about 35 percent each decade throughout the first half of the nineteenth century, reaching nearly ten million by 1820, and exceeding twenty-three million in 1850. Much of this growth was by immigration, with new streams of immigrants from Ireland and Germany joining the traditional flow from Britain. While many of the immigrants settled into the burgeoning cities of the East, there were many others, both new immigrants and established Americans and Canadian, moving west.

This was a time of trails. On news of fertile locations, trading opportunities, or gold strikes, prospective settlers would choose their trail to the West. The Santa Fe Trail carried thousands in the 1820s; the Oregon Trail was popular in the 1830s and 1840s. The California Trail through the north and the Oxbow Route to the south took settlers on routes thousands of miles long to their chosen destinations. All of these trails were very arduous to travel.

Certain settlers endured even more extreme privation. For example, the Church of Jesus Christ of Latter Day Saints, or Mormons, was just one of the religious groups that had inspired followers in the United States. Founded after a vision experienced by Joseph Smith in Palmyra, New York, in 1820, the church members were persecuted for their beliefs. After several moves westward the leader, Brigham Young, took thousands of followers on a trek from Nauvoo, Illinois, to Utah, where they established their Salt Lake settlement in 1847. This enormous, enforced journey was well planned and organized to minimize difficulties. The same could not be said when, subsequent to the Indian Removal Act, tribal peoples were forcibly removed from their homes in Florida, North Carolina, Georgia, Alabama, Tennessee, Mississippi, Wisconsin, Illinois, and Iowa territory to lands designated for their use, to the west of Arkansas. Four thousand Cherokee died on the Trail of Tears to the west. The American Indians who were removed in this way often found subsequently that they were deemed still not far enough away from white people. When their land became a worthwhile commodity, their rights to it had a tendency to fade away.

Eastern cities were growing rapidly, with New York City's population exceeding one million in 1860. Urban centers developed at major communications points on the routes to the west and south, some of them developing industries based on natural resources such as coal or iron deposits, others processing agricultural products, which were increasingly transported on the new railroads from the mid-nineteenth century. Chicago, founded only in 1833, was by 1860 one of the nation's largest cities. New technology had widespread impact. The cotton industry of Massachusetts, starting to organize as a factory system in the 1820s, had become one of the world's most productive by the 1840s. This development brought jobs and commercial profit, as well as deteriorating working conditions and despoiled environments.

Stories of the West had a ready market in the urban centers of the East. Promotional literature was distributed by entrepreneurs and by western cities, states, and territories. Adventure stories of the West, fictionalizing the exploits of real westerners such as "Kit" Carson, were very popular. In 1823, James Fenimore Cooper provided the West with some of its most lasting characters in *The Pioneers*, the first of a series of powerful and popular novels. The invention of the Morse telegraph in 1844 made it possible to receive instant news to elaborate the legends that were already developing about the West. With the annexation of Texas and the acquisition of vast new territories after the war with Mexico, the geographic and political integrity of what would become the forty-eight contiguous states was effectively established, and contemporary technology meant that the burgeoning population could read all about it.

REVOLUTION AND WAR OF INDEPENDENCE

The battle of Princeton, on January 3, 1777, where the Americans defeated three regiments of British troops.

The American Revolution of 1776 was the culmination of a series of irreconcilable differences between the American colonies and the government in London. While historians disagree on the major causes of the revolution, citing matters of ideology, economy, and the desire for autonomy and self-determination, the more immediate causes of the revolution resulted from specific acts imposed on the American colonies without their consent.

Prior to the Revolution, the colonies existed in a more or less autonomous condition. While legally they were to trade only with Britain in exchange for British protection against both Native Americans and other European powers, in practice the colonials largely protected themselves and traded with whomever they could.

For two years after the French and Indian War of 1754–1763, the British tried to tax the colonies to meet the costs of the war. The taxes levied by the British to help defray the cost of defense in America generated discontent. It was not so much due to the amount of tax as to the novelty of a distant parliament without American representation having the ability to impose a tax. Further acts sought to restrict the illegal American trade with the European powers conducted through the Caribbean.

With the resulting decline in trade, London soon repealed their acts, but within years tried to levy more taxes on tea. Samuel Adams led the resistance to this further tax by dumping copious amounts of tea in Boston Harbor in 1773. The British retaliated by imposing the Intolerable Acts, which closed Boston Harbor, replaced American administrators with British officials, and sought to limit the westward movement of the colonials by imposing the borders of Canada southward to the Ohio River.

The colonial response came with the creation of the First Continental Congress, which met in September 1774. The colonial powers realized there was a very close connection between their ability to trade and their political independence. The Québec Act of 1774 had effectively revived the conditions of inhibiting the westward movement of the colonials as had the Proclamation line of 1763. Westward movement was seen as essential, because trade to the east through the Caribbean had been curtailed.

In April 1775, the British tried to arrest American leaders Samuel Adams and John Hancock, and upon reaching Lexington eight Americans were killed, though no real battle took place. At Concord the fighting was more serious, resulting in an American victory. The following month the Second, more

Map labels

Americans withdraw to their original siege lines

Mystic River

Charlestown Neck

Charles River

Bunker Hill

Blockhouse

June 17: British attack Breed's Hill. After three assaults and over 1,000 casualties, they capture the hill.

Moulton's Hill

Breed's Hill

Midday, June 17: 2,200 British troops land

Charlestown

Dawn of June 17: British ships bombard American positions.

Boston Harbor

N

Dam
Mill pond

Boston
Copp's Hill

0   0.5 km
0   0.5 mile

BREED'S HILL, JUNE 1775

— British troops

→ British attack

— American militia

→ American withdrawal

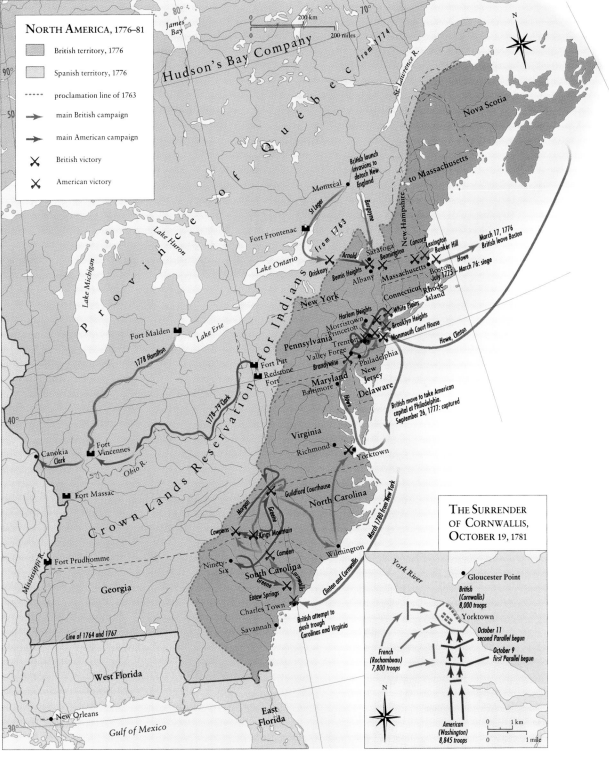

NORTH AMERICA, 1776–81

British territory, 1776

Spanish territory, 1776

proclamation line of 1763

main British campaign

main American campaign

British victory

American victory

Hudson's Bay Company

James Bay

Province of Quebec

from 1774

St. Lawrence R.

Nova Scotia

Lake Huron

Lake Michigan

Lake Erie

Lake Ontario

Fort Frontenac

from 1763

Fort Malden

1778 Hamilton

Montréal

St Leger

Burgoyne

British launch invasions to detach New England

New Hampshire to Massachusetts

Arnold

Saratoga

Bennington

Concord

Lexington

Bunker Hill

March 17, 1776 British leave Boston

Howe

Oriskany

Bemis Heights

Albany

Massachusetts

Boston July 1775 – March 76: siege

New York

Connecticut

Rhode Island

Harlem Heights

Morristown

Princeton

Trenton

White Plains

Brooklyn Heights

Monmouth Court House

Howe, Clinton

Pennsylvania

Valley Forge

Brandywine

Philadelphia

New Jersey

Fort Pitt

Redstone Fort

Maryland

Baltimore

Delaware

Howe

British move to take American capital at Philadelphia, September 26, 1777: captured

Crown Lands Reservation for Indians

Fort Vincennes

Canokia Clark

Ohio R.

1778-79 Clark

Fort Massac

Virginia

Richmond

Yorktown

Guildford Courthouse

North Carolina

Morgan

Greene

March 1780 from New York

Cowpens

Kings Mountain

Camden

Wilmington

Ninety-Six

South Carolina

Greene

Cornwallis

Eutaw Springs

Charles Town

Savannah

Clinton and Cornwallis

British attempt to push trough Carolinas and Virginia

Mississippi R.

Fort Prudhomme

Georgia

Line of 1764 and 1767

West Florida

New Orleans

East Florida

Gulf of Mexico

THE SURRENDER OF CORNWALLIS, OCTOBER 19, 1781

York River

Gloucester Point

British (Cornwallis) 8,000 troops

Yorktown

October 11 second Parallel begun

October 9 first Parallel begun

French (Rochambeau) 7,800 troops

American (Washington) 8,845 troops

0   1 km
0   1 mile

"A little
rebellion now
and then is a
good thing."
*Thomas
Jefferson*

radical, Continental Congress convened to search for European allies to assist the colonials fighting the British. The French were most eager to exact revenge following their defeat in the Seven Years' War.

Attempts by the Continental Congress to excite revolutionary fervor among the people of Québec met with hostility from the Anglophones and indifference from the Francophones. Nevertheless, considerable resources were spent on an American invasionary force which attacked Québec and Montréal. These efforts throughout the winter of 1775–1776 met with no success, and the American forces withdrew. In January 1776, the publication of Thomas Paine's pamphlet *Common Sense* had an immense impact on a highly literate population, reinvigorating the revolutionary spirit. By July 2, 1776, Congress accepted Thomas Jefferson's draft Declaration of Independence, which was proclaimed two days later. For the following seven years, the colonies engaged in many battles to secure their independence.

Within weeks, John Jay put forward his Model Treaty with France, which initiated several attempts to gain European support, principally from France, Spain, and Holland, against the British in the War of Independence.

The U.S.-French alliance signed in 1778 led ultimately to the last significant engagement between the alliance and the British at Yorktown from April to September 1781. Following that battle, the new British government under Lord Shelburne decided that a more effective strategy would be to recognize U.S. independence to mitigate the effects of an American-French alliance. The strategy assumed that because of the extensive economic ties between the United States and Britain, the States would move back toward the British in the economic sphere. The States negotiated the terms of their independence with Britain until late 1782, setting the borders of the United States in the north at the Great Lakes, in the south at the 31st parallel, and in the west at the Mississippi River. By 1783, U.S. independence had been won.

New York harbor, painted by an unknown artist about 1783. British ships crowded the anchorage for the last time in early December 1783, when the British commander Sir Guy Carlton evacuated his troops. New York had been a British stronghold since its capture by Sir William Howe in 1776.

NORTH AMERICA, c. 1796

- British territory
- United States
- Spanish territory
- disputed Spain–United States
- disputed Spain–Great Britain
- Russian Empire
- French territory

ARCTIC OCEAN

RUSSIAN EMPIRE

Bering Strait

Alaska

Northwest Territories

Hudson Bay

Rupert's Land (Hudson's Bay Company)

Vancouver Island

Greenland to Denmark

Arctic Circle

Upper Canada

Lower Canada

Newfoundland

Québec

Nova Scotia

Montréal

Northwest Territory

York

Detroit

Boston

UNITED STATES

New York

Philadelphia

St. Louis

Louisiana

San Francisco

N E W

Santa Fe

Los Angeles

San Diego

Tucson

El Paso

New Madrid

Louisville

Nashville

Williamsburg

New Bern

ATLANTIC OCEAN

Nacogdoches

Charleston

Savannah

PACIFIC OCEAN

Pensacola

St. Augustine

New Orleans

Monterey

Gulf of Mexico

Bahama Islands

Tropic of Cancer

S P A I N

León

Guadalajara

Havana

Mexico City

Veracruz

Cuba

Puerto Rico

British Honduras

Jamaica

Saint Domingue

Santo Domingo

N

0   400 km

0   400 miles

U.S. CONSTITUTION AND GOVERNMENT

"The only maxim of a free government ought to be to trust no man living with the power to endanger the pulic liberty."
John Adams

Ten years after the Declaration of Independence, the thirteen states were working together within the loose regulation of the Articles of Confederation. While this form of government did provide for a Continental Congress, this institution proved to be relatively toothless.

The states, acting to protect their own interests, were simultaneously establishing their own governments. They started making independent decisions that threatened to divide the Confederation with tariff barriers and competition. Nevertheless, the states did not always have the resources to manage their own affairs very successfully. Civil disorder threatened where the population was in economic distress, and in Massachusetts there was open rebellion.

At the same time the external threat to the new nation had not disappeared. Britain had a solid presence in North America, and was the world's largest naval power. At least some members of the British government were not distressed by the failure of the states to present a united front. Spain was well established in North America, and the states' relations with the indigenous peoples of North America were far from settled.

In the attempt to tackle some of these difficulties, Virginia called the Annapolis Conference (September 1786). The representatives, from five states, felt that wider representation was needed and drafted a call, later endorsed by the Continental Congress, for another meeting to discuss a much wider range of reforms.

The smaller states were suspicious that their interests might be ignored by a strengthened central government that could be dominated by the large states, and Rhode Island boycotted the Philadelphia Convention. All the other states sent delegations, and after a summer of debate thirty-nine delegates proposed a new Constitution for the United States of America on September 17, 1787. The terms of the Constitution required only nine states to ratify.

The first state to ratify was Delaware (December 7, 1787), followed in the same month by Pennsylvania and New Jersey, and in January and February 1788 by Georgia, Connecticut, and Massachusetts. In June, New Hampshire

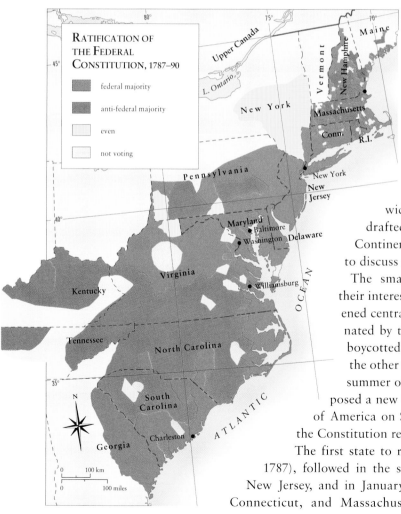

RATIFICATION OF THE FEDERAL CONSTITUTION, 1787–90

- federal majority
- anti-federal majority
- even
- not voting

became the ninth state to ratify, but New York and Virginia were still undecided, and it was clear that without these large and strategically placed states the new government would be unworkable.

The argument was intense, as Federalists (enthusiasts for the Constitution) and Antifederalists challenged each other in debate and in print. In June and July 1788, Virginia and New York ratified the Constitution. With North Carolina ratifying in November 1788, only Rhode Island was holding out against the new Constitution, finally agreeing in May 1790. Proposals heard during the ratification debates for the inclusion of greater citizen protections in the Constitution resulted in the proposal and eventual passage of the first ten Amendments to the Constitution, known as the Bill of Rights.

The institutions of government were quickly under way. George Washington was elected president, and was inaugurated in New York City on April 30, 1789, where the Senate and House of Representatives of the new government were already in operation. Maryland's suggestion that a new national capital be established on the banks of the Potomac, on land ceded to the federal government, led ultimately to the development of Washington, D.C., as the seat of the federal government.

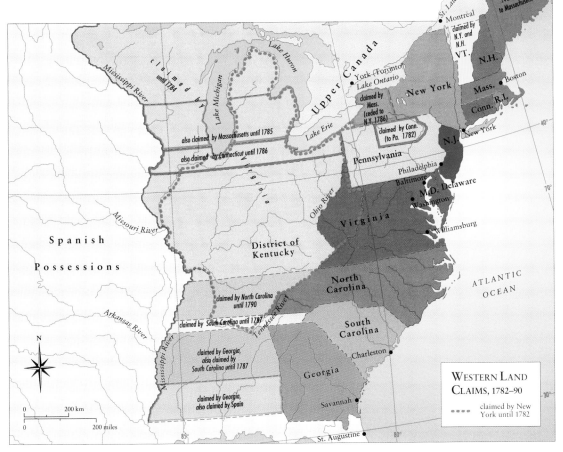

WESTERN LAND CLAIMS, 1782–90

claimed by New York until 1782

EARLY CANADA

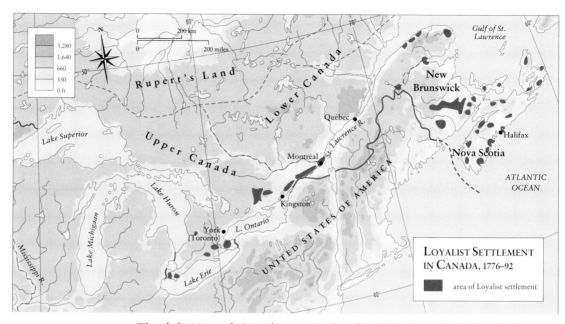

The definition of Canadian nationhood and its boundaries involved many actors. Britain, France, the native populations, the emerging United States, and the venture capitalists of the Hudson's Bay and North West companies all had an interest. The Treaty of Paris (1763), ending the Seven Year's War, eliminated France from colonial interest in North America, save for the islands of St. Pierre and Miquelon. In spite of the mass exit of Acadians from the Maritimes in the 1750s, there was left in Québec an established Francophone population. The Québec Act (1774) formalized arrangements, recognizing French civil law and freedom of religious practice for Catholics, while establishing English criminal law and confirming a system of rule by British crown appointees.

Some in the American War of Independence expected disaffected French and English speakers from the north to draw Canada along the same path, but there were few takers. But the war did change Canada. The Maritimes had a history of settlement, including the first popularly elected assembly, in Halifax (1758). About 30,000 British loyalists migrated north into the Maritimes, with thousands more migrating into other parts of British North America. French Canadians reacted by heading for the cultural guarantees of Québec. The provinces of Lower Canada and Upper Canada were created by the Constitutional Act (1791), Lower Canada being the more French, separated by a border on the Ottawa River.

American ambitions on Canada did not disappear. The economic development of Canada was slower than its southern neighbor; communications, especially into the western plains, were poor; and there was a steady migration from the United States into the cheaper lands in Canada. After the American declaration of war on Britain in 1812, many U.S. political leaders expected to take Canada. In spite of resentment in the Canadian provinces about their lack of autonomy, and continuing Francophone-Anglophone tension, this proved impossible.

Loyalists fought off the threat of being liberated by American republicanism, and much of the French Canadian population remained neutral. The Treaty of Ghent (1814) between Britain and the United States agreed to return to the prewar status quo, and was followed by the establishment of the Canadian–U.S. border along the 49th parallel, to the Rocky Mountains.

Canadian resentments were not addressed adequately, and in 1837, there were small but shocking rebellions, which led the British to appoint Lord Durham to investigate. His proposals, leading to the Act of Union (1840), combining Upper and Lower Canada into one, failed to comprehend or address French Canadian fears, but in recommending colonial self-government on domestic affairs he accelerated the move toward autonomy.

Tensions within the government of the united Upper and Lower (now called East and West) Canada led to virtual gridlock in spite of the skills of local moderate politicians, but in the provinces governors were conceding authority to locally elected legislations.

In 1844, when James K. Polk was elected to the U.S. presidency, his expansionist supporters in the west demanded a border of "Fifty-four forty or

EARLY CANADA, 1800–67

- original provinces of Canada, established by British North America Act, July 1867
- extent of British North America, including disputed territories (to 1846)
- territory disputed (or jointly occupied) by Britain with U.S.

Arctic Circle

Alaska to Russia

Beaufort Sea

Baffin Island

The North-western Territory

Great Bear Lake

Hudson's Bay Company until 1858

Stickeen Territory

1866 to British Columbia

Great Slave Lake

furthest extent of British claim

northern limit of U.S. claim

Hudson Bay

Rupert's Land

Newfoundland

British Columbia

Vancouver

1866 to British Columbia

1858 Crown colony

New Westminster

Victoria

1818-46 jointly occupied by Britain and U.S.

Oregon

1818 ceded by U.S.

1818 ceded by Britain

1842 ceded by U.S.

L. Superior

St. John's

Québec

St. Lawrence R.

1842 ceded by U.S.

Québec

New Brunswick

1842 ceded by Britain

Nova Scotia

Halifax

1842 ceded by Britain

Ontario

Toronto

Montreal

L. Michigan

Huron

L. Erie

L. Ontario

ATLANTIC OCEAN

UNITED STATES

0   400 km

0   400 miles

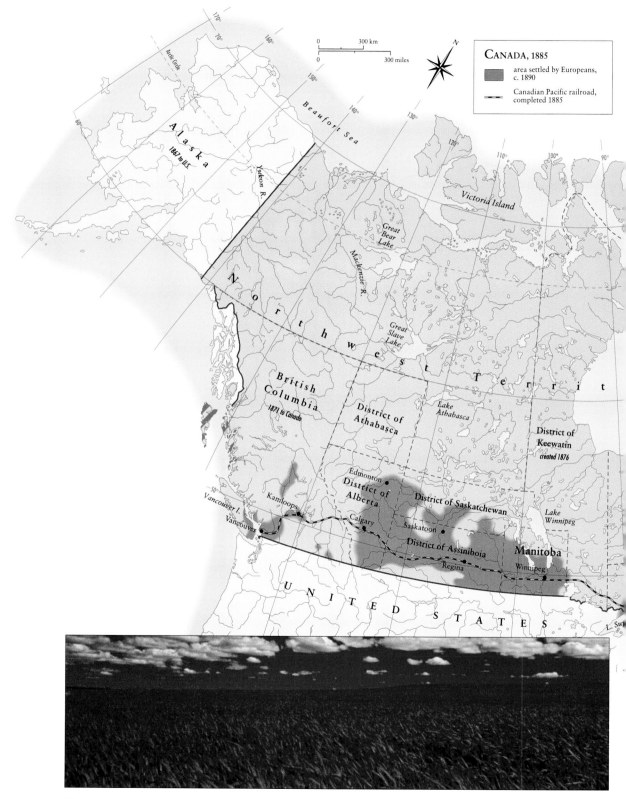

CANADA, 1885

area settled by Europeans, c. 1890

Canadian Pacific railroad, completed 1885

Alaska 1867 to US

Beaufort Sea

Yukon R.

Victoria Island

Great Bear Lake

Mackenzie R.

Great Slave Lake

North West Territorit

British Columbia 1871 to Canada

District of Athabasca

Lake Athabasca

District of Keewatin created 1876

Edmonton

District of Alberta

District of Saskatchewan

Lake Winnipeg

Kamloops

Calgary

Saskatoon

Vancouver I.

Vancouver

District of Assiniboia

Manitoba

Regina

Winnipeg

L. Su

U N I T E D   S T A T E S

fight." The Oregon Treaty (1846) dismissed these claims, extending the 49th parallel to the Pacific, with a dip south to include Vancouver Island in Canada. Shortly after, in 1858, the discovery of gold in British Columbia confirmed the importance of this area for Canada, stimulated immigration to the Pacific Coast region, and prompted the political upgrading of this territory to full colonial status. The outbreak of the U.S. Civil War (1861) increased Canadian fears of annexation across the huge unguarded border between Canada and the United States. A sudden British shift toward the idea of federation in Canada appeared simultaneously to address the internal tensions and the external threat.

The British North America Act (1867) set up the Dominion of Canada, with Québec, Ontario, New Brunswick, and Nova Scotia as members. In 1869, huge tracts of western lands were purchased from the Hudson's Bay Company by the government, after which Manitoba and the Northwest Territories (1870) joined the Dominion. British Columbia was added in 1871, lured by Ottawa's promise that a transcontinental railway be built (completed in 1885). The Maritimes had not been wholeheartedly in favor of sacrificing their independent colony status— Nova Scotia had been a founder member in spite of considerable local opposition, with Prince Edward Island and Newfoundland declining to join at first. The former joined in 1873, but Newfoundland held out until 1949.

The availability of thousands of square miles of cheap land in the prairie provinces of Canada attracted settlers from established communities in the East and many European states. Many also came from the United States, attracted by cheaper land values. It was this fusion of people that transformed the region into the huge wheat producer seen today, and the growing population of the western provinces would affect the nation's political future.

LOUISIANA PURCHASE

The elections of 1800 saw a transition of power from the Federalists to the Democratic-Republicans, allowing Thomas Jefferson to become the third U.S. president. Jefferson envisioned the expansion of the United States as far and wide as possible, creating a nation with a similar culture, language, and political system. His most immediate concern was to gain the Mississippi valley, but ultimately he also sought land west to the Pacific; south to the Floridas and Cuba, which he hoped to obtain from the Spanish; and perhaps extending to Central America, where a canal might be built across the isthmus.

As Jefferson inaugurated his presidency, Spanish power waned, and Spain ultimately surrendered to the French, later selling them the Louisiana territories. Under Napoleon, the French immediately envisioned the prospects of rebuilding a new French empire in the New World. The Spanish, however, still controlled the city of New Orleans, and closed down trade with the United States. Jefferson let it be known in France, through communication with the U.S. representative, that the day France acquired New Orleans would be the day that the United States would be forced to go into closer cooperation with the British fleet.

Information concerning territories to the west was sketchy at best. In this detail from A Map of the British Empire in North America by Henry Popple, drawn in 1733, he relied almost exclusively on French material gathered over the previous sixty years.

With the French acquisition of the city in 1803, Jefferson and his Secretary of State immediately began the process of persuading them to sell it. Madison's idea was that the Louisiana Territory would become a liability if the French did not need the territory to feed the slave population in Santo Domingo engaged in producing sugar and coffee. The United States began to assist the slave revolt in Haiti under Toussaint L'Ouverture as a tactic to gain control of Louisiana. Though L'Ouverture was captured, the revolt was still successful.

Jefferson then used the clearance of the Native Americans to his advantage. The brutal but effective policy of clearing the Native American tribes from the Midwest forced them into Napoleon's jurisdiction. The cleared areas under U.S. control allowed the dominantly white population of the Midwest to conduct a more undisturbed attack on the French in the lower Mississippi area.

By 1803, Napoleon had learned of Jefferson's authorization from Congress to raise a militia to attack the area. James Monroe, future president of the United States, had set sail to Paris to negotiate the purchase of New Orleans and the Floridas. The day before his arrival, the French indicated to the American representative, Robert Livingstone, that the French wanted to get rid of their North American territories. In preparation for the war against the British, Napoleon did not want to deal with the potential problems of various wars in America or a potential U.S. alliance with Britain. Though Livingstone and Monroe's instructions were to purchase New Orleans and the Floridas for $10 million, they did not hesitate to accept an offer to purchase New Orleans and unspecified territory to the north for $15 million. This additional land encompassed the territory between New Orleans and the expanse between the Mississippi River and the Rocky Mountains.

The treaty was signed in April 1803, and ultimately when the transfer took place in December, the United States acquired 50,000 new citizens of French, Creole, and Spanish descent, and also 150,000 Native Americans without their consent. The Louisiana Purchase doubled the size of the United States. Many

LOUISIANA PURCHASE, 1803

United States, 1783

Louisiana purchase, 1803 (natural boundary)

joint occupation with Great Britain

ceded by U.S. to Great Britain, 1818

ceded by Great Britain to U.S., 1818

ceded by Spain to U.S., 1819

Spanish empire after 1819

Spanish treaty line of 1819

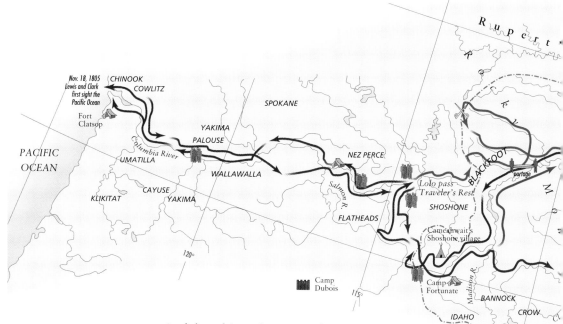

recognized that ultimately it was only a matter of time before the United States would become an equal among the great powers of the world. Napoleon indicated that he had "just given England a maritime rival that sooner or later will lay low her pride."

President Jefferson, anxious to gain a clear understanding of the Louisiana territories, had already asked Congress for funding for an expedition up the Missouri River on January 18, 1803. Meriwether Lewis, a young army captain, and William Clark were appointed co-captains of the expedition. On May 14, 1804, the two captains, together with 38 men forming the Corps of Discovery, set off from Wood River on the Mississippi. After suffering every kind of hardship, one year and six months later they sighted the Pacific Ocean on November 18, 1805. Their return journey took six months. They were back east in September 1806 bearing notebooks and maps crammed with information on the new lands to the west.

The Louisiana Purchase produced a constitutional crisis. There was no direct constitutional provision for such an acquisition of additional territory, though there was the scope for the admission of new states. Some states felt that the acquisition of territory would threaten the balance and the nature of the U.S. system. New England considered seceding from the Union, with the support of Jefferson's vice president, Aaron Burr. The solution that emerged was to administer the newly acquired territory by presidential decree. This was an expansion of the powers of the president and central governnment, contrary to Jefferson's former stance as a strict constitutionalist. States would be formed from the territory as it gained sufficient population.

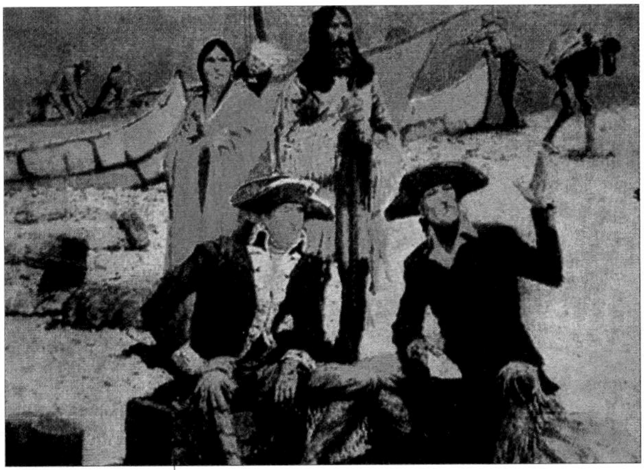

Lewis and Clark plan their next move. Standing behind them is Sacajawea, a Shoshone interpreter, carrying her infant son. From a painting by Frederic Remington.

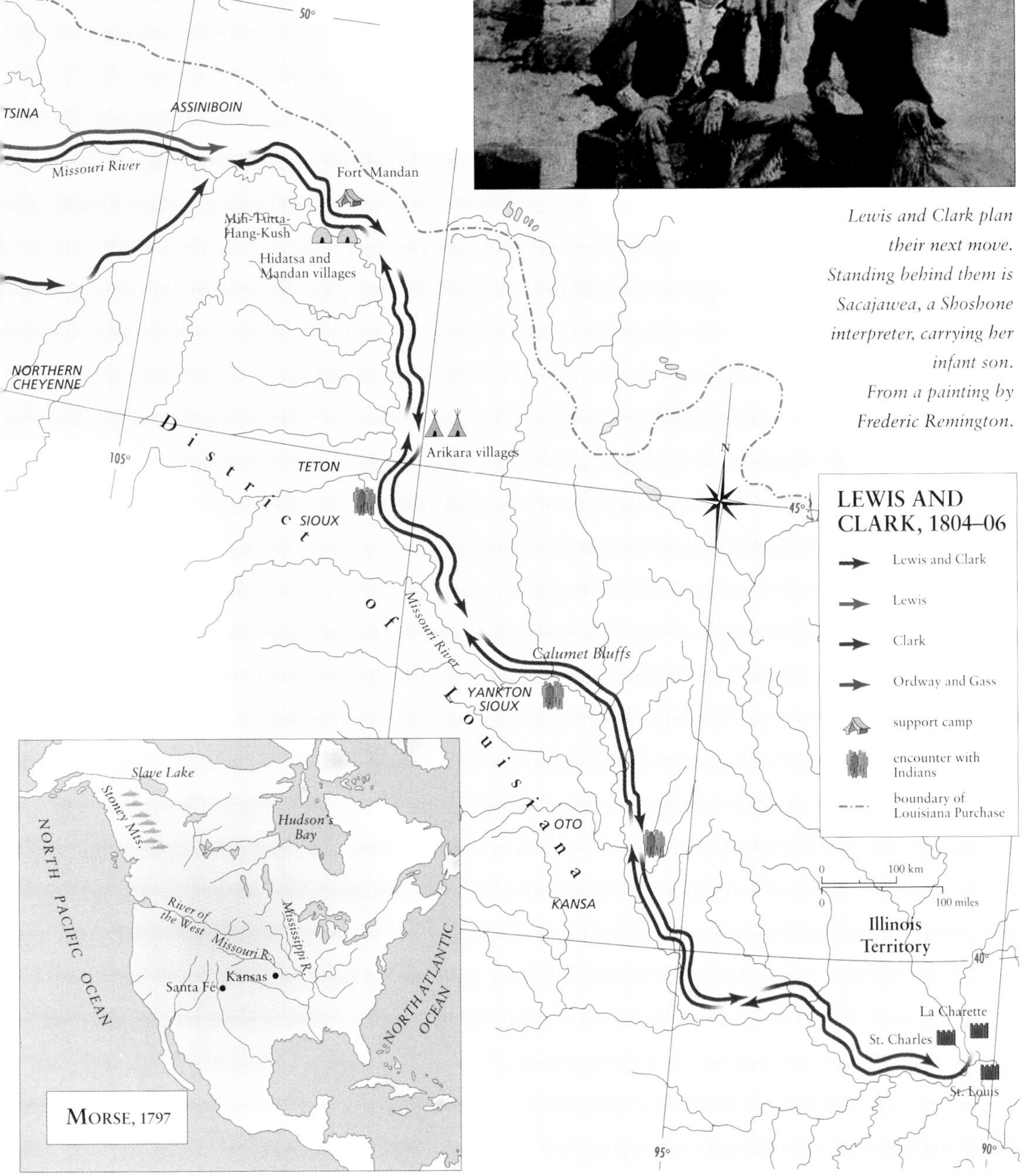
LEWIS AND CLARK, 1804–06
Lewis and Clark
Lewis
Clark
Ordway and Gass
support camp
encounter with Indians
boundary of Louisiana Purchase
0 100 km
0 100 miles
a n d
50°
TSINA
ASSINIBOIN
Missouri River
Fort Mandan
Mih-Tutta-Hang-Kush
Hidatsa and Mandan villages
NORTHERN CHEYENNE
District of Louisiana
105°
TETON
SIOUX
Arikara villages
N
45°
Missouri River
Calumet Bluffs
YANKTON SIOUX
OTO
KANSA
Illinois Territory
40°
La Charette
St. Charles
St. Louis
95°
90°
Slave Lake
Stoney Mts.
Hudson's Bay
NORTH PACIFIC OCEAN
River of the West
Missouri R.
Mississippi R.
Kansas
Santa Fé
NORTH ATLANTIC OCEAN
Morse, 1797

WAR OF 1812

The outcome of the War of 1812 was a tremendous diplomatic victory for the United States, despite the results of the key engagements and the threats to the Union by the Federalists opposed to the war.

The war resulted from the broader conflict between Britain and France and a series of issues accurately reflected by Madison in his War Message of June 1812. The United States had traded with both Britain and France, but each of these two powers wanted to prevent the other's gaining from the advantages of trade with the United States. Ultimately in June 1812, President James Madison chose to declare war on Great Britain because it seemed to pose a greater threat to U.S. interests, as perceived at the time. Not only could the British act more concertedly against U.S. shipping; they were also seen as inciting the Native Americans against the United States. In addition, Britain posed a greater threat to U.S. commerce in the bid to exert more influence in Latin America, which at this point was wresting itself away from the Spanish empire.

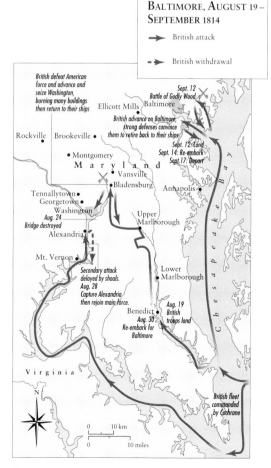

OPERATIONS AROUND WASHINGTON AND BALTIMORE, AUGUST 19 – SEPTEMBER 1814

→ British attack

--→ British withdrawal

British defeat American force and advance and seize Washington, burning many buildings then return to their ships

Ellicott Mills

Sept. 12
Battle of Godly Wood
Baltimore

British advance on Baltimore, strong defenses convince them to retire back to their ships

Sept. 12: Land
Sept. 14: Re-embark
Sept. 17: Depart

Rockville

Brookeville

Montgomery

M a r y l a n d

Vansville
Bladensburg

Annapolis

Tennallytown
Georgetown
Washington
Aug. 24
Bridge destroyed
Alexandria

Upper
Marlborough

Mt. Vernon

Secondary attack delayed by shoals.
Aug. 28
Capture Alexandria then rejoin main force.

Lower
Marlborough

Benedict
Aug. 30
Re-embark for Baltimore

Aug. 19
British troops land

C h e s a p e a k e   B a y

V i r g i n i a

N

British fleet commanded by Cochrane

0   10 km
0   10 miles

In his War Message, Madison cited the practice of "impressment" (forced service) of U.S. sailors by the British Navy; accused the British of operating "pretended blockades" and violating U.S. commerce against international laws; decried the British "Orders in Council," which violated U.S. commercial interests and maintained a British monopoly in commerce and navigation; and accused the British of inciting Native American violence against U.S. interests. There was a seeming contradiction in the congressional vote for war. The southern and western Republicans favored war during a period of commercial recession, while the northern Federalists, engaged more extensively with maritime trade with the British, voted against war. Despite this, the emphasis in Madison's message was on the various issues relating to the maritime concerns.

Historians have speculated on whether the war could have been avoided had communications between London and Washington been more speedy. The British repealed the Orders in Council on June 16, 1812, but still the other issues remained, and the opportunity to seize Canada and perhaps make it an additional U.S. state were too tempting.

Despite three initial victories for the United States on the ocean during the summer of 1812, the British soon coordinated themselves and controlled the coastal regions with their numerically far superior fleet. The land war took place in three distinct phases

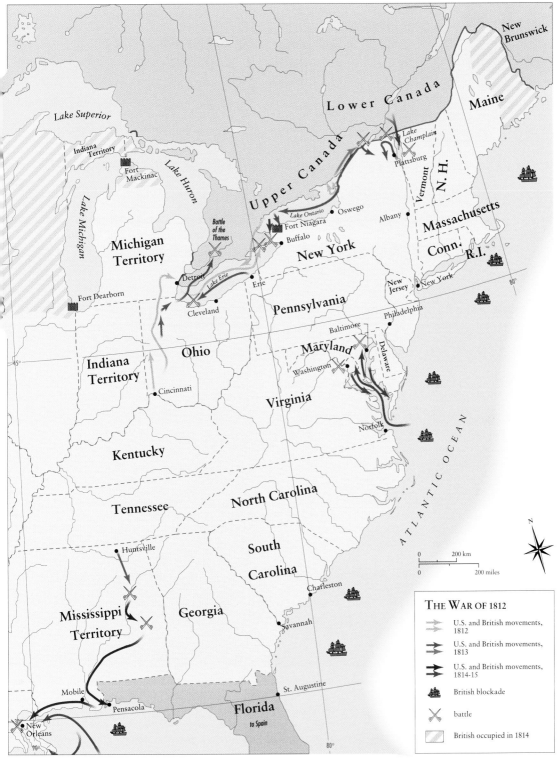

Lake Superior

Indiana
Territory

Fort
Mackinac

Lake Huron

Lower Canada

Maine

New
Brunswick

Upper Canada

Lake Champlain

Plattsburg

N. H.

Vermont

Lake Ontario

Oswego

Albany

Massachusetts

Lake Michigan

Michigan
Territory

Battle
of the
Thames

Fort Niagara

Buffalo

New York

Conn.

R.I.

Detroit

Lake Erie

Erie

New
Jersey

New York

80°

Cleveland

Pennsylvania

Fort Dearborn

Ohio

Philadelphia

Baltimore

Maryland

Delaware

Indiana
Territory

Washington

Virginia

45°

Cincinnati

Norfolk

ATLANTIC OCEAN

Kentucky

Tennessee

North Carolina

Huntsville

South
Carolina

Charleston

Mississippi
Territory

Georgia

Savannah

N

0   200 km

0   200 miles

THE WAR OF 1812

→ U.S. and British movements, 1812

→ U.S. and British movements, 1813

→ U.S. and British movements, 1814-15

British blockade

✕ battle

British occupied in 1814

Mobile

Pensacola

Florida

St. Augustine

to Spain

New
Orleans

70°

80°

both temporally and geographically, between 1812 and 1815.

The first and most protracted conflict occurred along the U.S.–Canadian border, from around the Great Lakes in the west to as far north as Lake Champlain. These conflicts took place between July 1812 and the fall of 1814, with major battles at Fort Dearborn (now Chicago), the Thames River, Fort Niagara, and Plattsburgh. The U.S. forces met considerable resistance by Canadians and Loyalists who had moved to Canada after the Revolution. The second area of engagement involved a British amphibious attack on Washington and Baltimore in August 1814. The British routed the much larger U.S. forces, ultimately burning the White House and other state buildings; President Monroe retreated west toward the Appalachians.

Again, had communications been speedier, the final phase of battle would have been unnecessary. The British attack on New Orleans in January 1815 was successfully repelled by General Andrew Jackson (later president between 1829 and 1837). The battle was unnecessary, because in December 1814 the United States and Britain had concluded their negotiations with the Treaty of Ghent in Belgium, on the basis of the *status quo ante bellum*. The final battle, however, provided a boost for the morale of the United States and for the career of Andrew Jackson.

The results of the war prevented the threatened cessation of Hartford in its search for better trading relations with Britain. It also allowed the United States to concentrate on its westward expansion and the creation of the so-called "Empire of Liberty." With its expanding territory, the Union would prove considerably more difficult to maintain in the future.

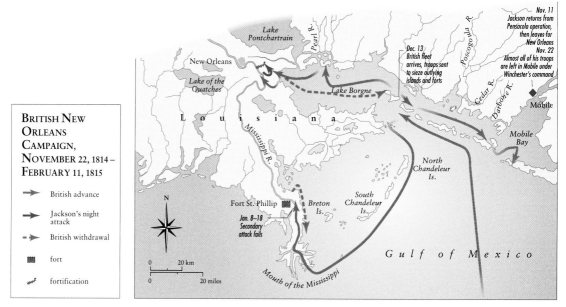

BRITISH NEW ORLEANS CAMPAIGN, NOVEMBER 22, 1814 – FEBRUARY 11, 1815

→ British advance

➡ Jackson's night attack

⇢ British withdrawal

▨ fort

〰 fortification

Andrew Jackson, born in South Carolina in 1767, first became an Indian fighter, then military leader. He defeated the British at the battle of New Orleans, January 1815. His popularity eventually led him to be elected president in 1829.

INDIAN REMOVAL

"They possessed neither tents nor wagons, but only their arms and some provisions. I saw them embark to pass the mighty river. Never will that solemn spectacle fade from my remembrance. No cry, no sob, was heard among the assembled crowd; all were silent."
Alexis de Tocqueville,
from
Democracy in America

The antebellum United States looked to resolve the status of Native Americans within the republic. This debate was intrinsically linked to other aspects of American society, including westward movement of settlers and the rapidly developing idea of the superiority of the white "race."

Federal government had been the key agent in preventing blatant abuse of Indian rights, and if only partially successful had at least attempted to bring some measure of justice. A number of eastern politicians, such as Thomas Jefferson, displayed great sympathy toward the indigenous peoples and believed they could be incorporated into American society in time. Of course, states on the Atlantic seaboard had subjugated their Indian populations many years beforehand, perhaps allowing such support, but nonetheless, Congress did prevent western states from taking unilateral action to satisfy land-hungry settlers. That changed with the election of Andrew Jackson in 1828. Jackson was a popular veteran of the War of 1812 and had earned a reputation as a renowned Indian-fighter after leading a vicious campaign against the Creeks and Seminoles. During the 1830s, successive administrations worked hand in hand with state governments in a policy of forced Indian removal. Assimilation was replaced by exclusion.

The Indian Removal Act, passed on May 28, 1830, set out the basic parameters of the new policy. It provided funds for the relocation of all Indian tribes west of the Mississippi, protection for the journey, and land in the new Indian Territory, to be held in perpetuity. On the face of it, the offer might have appeared reasonable. However, it ignored the attachment to land and environment that was central to Indian culture, and the fact that tribes had inhabited the area for thousands of years. It also ignored the changes that native peoples had already made in response to the settlers. The "Five Civilized Tribes" (Choctaw, Chickasaw, Creek, Cherokee and Seminole) had adapted their lifestyles to include many aspects of white society, including a form of writing, settled farming, the use of school for their children, a more hierarchical political system, and widespread conversion to Christianity.

The Cherokees took their opposition to the Supreme Court in two landmark cases. In *Cherokee Nation v. Georgia* (1831), John Ross argued that Georgia had no jurisdiction over Indians who had occupied the land from time immemorial. Chief Justice John Marshall's response was ambiguous, seeming to agree with the Cherokee leader's reasoning, but denying the right of a "domestic dependent nation" to bring the case to the Supreme Court. A year later, *Worcester v. Georgia* clarified the position as Marshall supported the Cherokee as a "distinct political community," entitled to federal protection, and not subject to state law. Andrew Jackson's response reportedly was to say: "John Marshall has made his decision; now let him enforce it," exposing any pretense of justice as a sham, as remaining tribes in the East were forced to leave.

Thus began one of the most shameful episodes in American history. Treaty negotiators, state officials, and, in the final instance, the army used coercive measures to evict Indians. In the Old Northwest, the Sac and Fox opposed relocation but were defeated in the Black Hawk War of 1832. The Seminoles also violently resisted in a guerrilla war (1835–1842) in Florida that cost the federal government $20 million.

However, most simply resigned themselves to their inevitable fate and set out for the Indian Territory (present-day Oklahoma). The Cherokee aptly called their 800-mile journey the "Trail of Tears." Of the 18,500 who set off in 1838, 4,000 lost their lives due to inadequate protection, a lack of provisions, and appalling winter conditions.

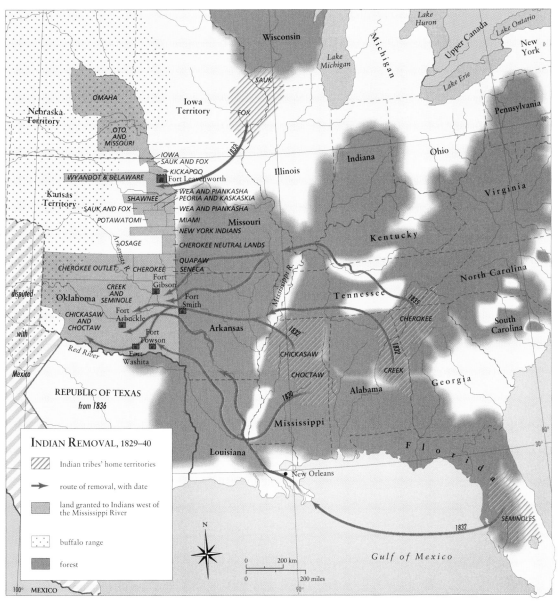

INDIAN REMOVAL, 1829–40

Indian tribes' home territories

route of removal, with date

land granted to Indians west of the Mississippi River

buffalo range

forest

THE MEXICAN–AMERICAN WAR

The combination of Mexico's internal weakness and the migration of large numbers of American nationals into the Texas territory soon produced a crisis. In 1836, U.S. settlers in Texas rebelled against the central Mexican government and, after defeating the army of General Santa Anna, declared independence. The status of the newly independent republic of Texas immediately created tension and friction in the relationship between Mexico and the United States, as Mexico refused to recognize the Texan government. In the United States the debate raged about whether the slave-holding territory of Texas should be annexed. The eventual decision by the American government to annex Texas in 1845 put the two nations on a collision course toward war.

The entry of U.S. troops into the disputed area between the Nueces River and the Rio Grande was the catalyst for war as Mexican forces counterattacked and the conflict unfolded. In May 1846, Washington declared war and the conflict known today in Mexico as the War of the North American Invasion began.

While neither nation had been fully prepared for war, Mexico, with its poorly organized and poorly supplied armed forces, was at the greater disadvantage. Over time, U.S. forces launched their attacks from widely dispersed theaters of operations. In August 1846, U.S. Navy units in the Pacific seized key ports in California which effectively brought that region under their control. General Zachary Taylor's army in September 1846 launched its campaign directed at Monterrey and defeated General Santa Anna's army at Buena Vista the following February. Colonel Stephen Kearny's forces seized Santa Fe in August 1846 and then struck out to join the U.S. naval forces at San Diego, an action that ended Mexican resistance in California.

In 1847, the war was reaching a decisive stage. The army of General Winfield Scott started a major thrust in March 1847, when it captured the city of Veracruz and then, on the march to Mexico City, defeated Santa Anna's forces. The latter victory cleared the way for Scott's army to enter Mexico City in September 1847, and the Mexican government was forced to flee to Queretaro.

A stunned and embittered Mexico was shocked by the outcome of the war, while the United States was well on the way toward the complete realization of its "manifest destiny" dream.

By February 1848, in the Treaty of Guadalupe Hidalgo, Mexico ceded vast amounts of its territory, and the United States increased its territory by twenty percent.

MEXICO, 1822–53

- Mexican republic, 1822
- territories lost, 1823
- effective control lost, 1836
- territories lost, 1848
- territory sold, 1853

United States

MEXICO

Dallas
Texas

Mexico City

British
Honduras

Mosquito Coast
to Britain

Panama

REPUBLIC
OF
GREATER
COLOMBIA
to 1830

N

0   500 km

0   500 miles

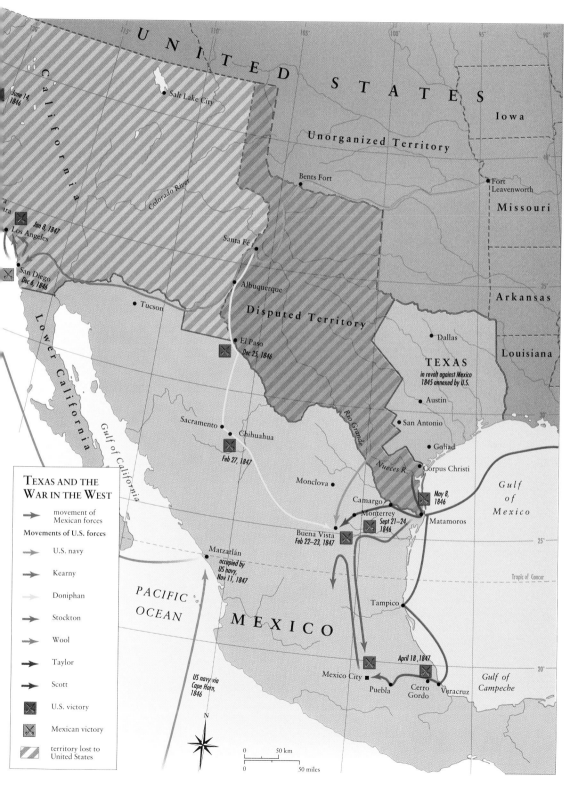

TEXAS AND THE WAR IN THE WEST

→ movement of Mexican forces

Movements of U.S. forces

→ U.S. navy

→ Kearny

→ Doniphan

→ Stockton

→ Wool

→ Taylor

→ Scott

⊠ U.S. victory

⊠ Mexican victory

⬚ territory lost to United States

UNITED STATES

California

June 14 1846

Salt Lake City

Unorganized Territory

Iowa

Bents Fort

Fort Leavenworth

Missouri

Colorado River

Santa Fé

Jan 8, 1847
Los Angeles

San Diego
Dec 6, 1846

Albuquerque

Tucson

Disputed Territory

Dallas

El Paso
Dec 25, 1846

Lower California

Gulf of California

Sacramento

Chihuahua

Feb 27, 1847

TEXAS
in revolt against Mexico 1845 annexed by U.S.

Louisiana

Arkansas

Austin

San Antonio

Goliad

Rio Grande

Nueces R.

Corpus Christi

Monclova

Camargo

May 8, 1846

Monterrey
Sept 21–24, 1846

Matamoros

Buena Vista
Feb 22–23, 1847

Gulf
of
Mexico

Matzatlán
occupied by US navy, Nov 11, 1847

PACIFIC
OCEAN

MEXICO

US navy via
Cape Horn,
1846

Tropic of Cancer

Tampico

April 18, 1847

Mexico City

Puebla

Cerro
Gordo

Veracruz

Gulf of
Campeche

N

0   50 km

0   50 miles

MANIFEST DESTINY AND THE WEST

Determined to find a home in the west is this Mormon family, photographed in the 1860s.

"... the fulfill-
ment of our
manifest destiny
to overspread
the continent
alloted by
Providence for
the free develop-
ment of our
yearly multiply-
ing millions."
*John L.
O'Sullivan,*
in *Democratic
Review*

Though U.S. expansion was not linear and uninterrupted, there was constant pressure for more land and access to western ports. By the 1830s, significant numbers of Americans moved into western areas—in particular, to Texas and Oregon. By the end of the 1840s, Texas was admitted to the Union, the United States had doubled in size, and Mexico had lost one-third of its territory in the Mexican-American War.

The term "manifest destiny" was coined by the editor of the *Democratic Review* to describe the U.S. westward movement. In 1845, he argued that opposition to the annexation of Texas might hinder "the fulfilment of our manifest destiny to overspread the continent allotted by Providence for the free development of our yearly multiplying millions." Historian Walter LaFeber points out that the darker side of this belief in providential destiny was that the United States had to "expand or die" to accommodate the increasing population.

American settlers had started moving into Texas in the early 1820s, led by Moses Austin. By the 1830s, the American numbers had increased significantly, in some areas outnumbering the local Mexican population. With the threat of losing control of the region, the Mexican government under Santa Anna centralized power in Mexico City. The Texas settlers resisted the move, and in 1836 established the independent Republic of Texas, recognized by the United States under President Andrew Jackson, but contested by the Mexicans. Though Jackson and his successor, Martin Van Buren, wanted to annex the republic, they first had to generate sufficient domestic support, because the addition of Texas would favor the Southern slave states and upset the balance within the Union. After almost ten years of independence, Texas was granted statehood in 1845.

Apart from the movement into Texas, Americans had moved into most western regions of the continent from Oregon to California, their families loaded onto 'Conestoga' wagons. They rolled across the great American desert to desirable lands in the west, via well worn routes like the Oregon and Mormon trails. Later after the completion of the first rail link many others made the journey courtesy of the Central Pacific and Union Pacific transcontinental railroads. The United States sought both the lands of the West and the ports of California, important for the potential trade with China and the Far East. The more peaceful U.S. efforts to gain control of the West from the Mexicans met with failure. Eventually, President James Polk, sent U.S. troops under General Zachary Taylor to occupy the disputed territory.

Finally, pressure from business groups interested in controlling a southern railroad route to the West Coast resulted in the Gadsden Purchase, a stretch of territory which became the southern part of Arizona and New Mexico. The purchase was completed in 1853.

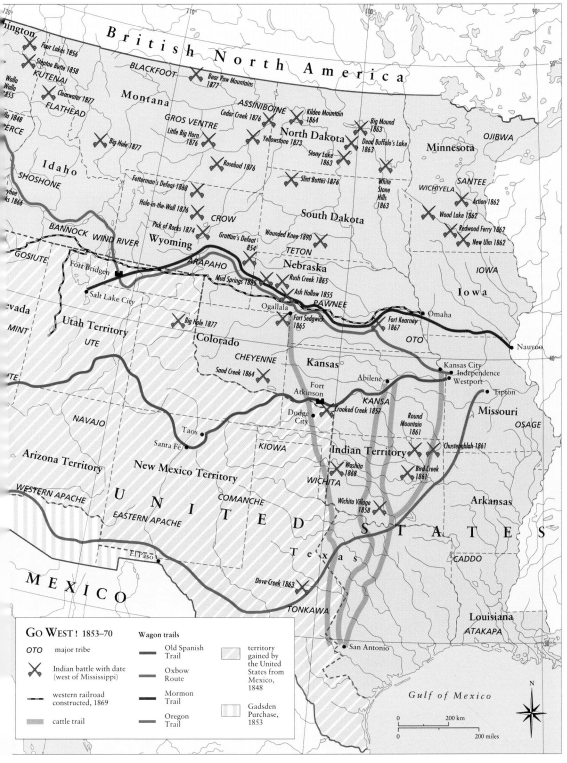

British North America

Four Lakes 1856
Steptoe Butte 1858
KUTENAI
Walla Walla 1855
Clearwater 1877
FLATHEAD
la 1848
PERCE

BLACKFOOT

Bear Paw Mountains 1877

Montana

ASSINIBOINE

Cedar Creek 1876

Kildee Mountain 1864

Big Mound 1863

GROS VENTRE
Little Big Horn 1876
Yellowstone 1873
North Dakota
Dead Buffalo's Lake 1863

OJIBWA

Idaho
SHOSHONE

Big Hole 1877

Fetterman's Defeat 1868

Rosebud 1876

Stony Lake 1863

Minnesota

Slim Buttes 1876

White Stone Hills 1863

SANTEE

WICHIYELA

Action 1862

yhee
1866

Hole-in-the-Wall 1876

CROW

South Dakota

Wood Lake 1862

BANNOCK WIND RIVER
Pick of Rocks 1874

Wyoming

Grattan's Defeat 854

Wounded Knee 1890

Redwood Ferry 1862
New Ulm 1862

GOSIUTE

Fort Bridger

ARAPAHO

TETON

Nebraska

IOWA

Mud Springs 1865
Rush Creek 1865

Iowa

vada
MINT

Salt Lake City

Ash Hollow 1855

Utah Territory

Ogallala

PAWNEE

Omaha

Fort Sedgwick 1865

Fort Kearney 1867

Nauvoo

TE

UTE

Big Hole 1877

Colorado

OTO

CHEYENNE

Kansas

Kansas City
Independence
Westport

Sand Creek 1864

Abilene

Tipton

Fort Atkinson

KANSA

Crooked Creek 1857

Dodge City

Round Mountain 1861

Missouri

Taos

OSAGE

Santa Fé

KIOWA

Indian Territory

Chustenahlah 1861

Arizona Territory

New Mexico Territory

Washita 1868

WICHITA

Bird Creek 1861

Arkansas

WESTERN APACHE

COMANCHE

U N I T E D

EASTERN APACHE

Wichita Village 1858

S T A T E S

El Paso

MEXICO

T e x a s

CADDO

Dove Creek 1863

TONKAWA

Louisiana

ATAKAPA

San Antonio

Gulf of Mexico

N

PART III: THE SOUTH AND THE CIVIL WAR

The road past Harpers Ferry engine house, the scene of John Brown's slave rebellion, which was brought to a bloody end by the United States Marines, commanded by Lieutenant Colonel Robert E. Lee.

When considering the South and the Civil War, the institution of slavery is of critical importance. Slave labor adapted smoothly to the transition from tobacco to cotton in the late eighteenth century, stimulated by Eli Whitney's invention of the cotton gin in 1793. This simple device, separating seeds from cotton fibers, immensely increased the profitability of cotton and ensured not only the survival of slavery but its rapid growth. Slavery became the foundation of a distinctive society that grew apart from other regions. It took a bloody Civil War (1861–1865) costing 620,000 lives to force abolition. Unsurprisingly, then, the adjustment to a free society during the eras of Reconstruction (1865–1877) and the New South (post-1877) was not easy.

Initially a response to economic needs, slavery had an impact that went much deeper. Historians have pointed out how the South changed from a society with slaves to a slave society during the era of the American Revolution. This subtle shift in emphasis reflects the manner in which slavery increasingly influenced all aspects of life in the antebellum South.

Most obviously, slavery defined race relations. Whites were constantly reminded of what it meant to be free. This had not always been the case—many traced their ancestry back to indentured servants—but over time they gained a heightened appreciation of freedom and came to associate blacks with bondage. Southern politicians often stated that because slaves carried out essential manual labor, all white Southerners enjoyed equality and harmony, in contrast to social unrest and frustration in the North. As South Carolinian James Henry Hammond proclaimed in the Senate, "there must be a class to perform the menial duties. It constitutes the very mud-sill of society. Fortunately for the South we have found a race adapted to that purpose." In effect, it was argued that the South had just two classes, slave and free. Of course, this was an exaggerated claim. There were actually 250,000 free blacks in the South who, although not legally bound to any slaveholder, were not regarded as equal citizens able to participate in Southern white society.

Nonslaveholders did not uniformly support or oppose slavery. Southern opposition to slavery by nonslaveholders stemmed primarily from economic concerns; many nonslaveholders feared the potential competition of slave labor. Other nonslaveholders supported slavery with racist arguments, explicit in Hammond's "mud-sill" statement, which were voiced incessantly after 1830 in the defense of slavery.

Social status was defined by slaveholding. The elite planter class received a disproportionate share of wealth and dominated Southern politics, which might have led to conflict with the less affluent majority. However, the South's labor system reduced friction among whites, as the vast majority were independent landowners, engaged in similar economic pursuits. A high level of land ownership and political participation reflected that essential unity. Moreover, the promise of slave ownership extended to many whites, as prosperous yeoman farmers strove to climb the social ladder. Other groups were left largely independent and untroubled by slaveholders, as the South was divided into distinct geographical regions.

Thus, Southern opposition to slavery, which had been conspicuous in the upper South at the turn of the 1800s, became isolated and impotent by the late antebellum period. Although considerable potential for conflict existed, it was mitigated by a host of circumstances. Underpinning the factors outlined above was a powerful proslavery argument advanced by politicians, lawyers, intellectuals, physicians, scientists, writers, and even clergymen. Drawing upon history, religion, science, economics, and politics, proslavery spokesmen presented a comprehensive justification of the peculiar institution. The most damaging element, in the long run, was the dissemination of a racist ideology positing immutable biological differences, which led to the widespread belief in black inferiority and white superiority.

The proslavery argument responded to attacks on slavery by abolitionists, who played a key role in increasing sectional discord. William Lloyd Garrison began publishing the *Liberator* newspaper in Boston in 1831. His first editorial set the tone of the abolitionist message: "I am in earnest – I will not equivocate – I will not excuse – I will not retreat a single inch – AND I WILL BE HEARD." That uncompromising message bluntly stated that slaveholding was a sin and called for immediate emancipation. Garrison was supported by free blacks, philanthropists, and wealthy reformers such as the Tappan brothers, who collectively formed the American Anti-Slavery Society in 1833.

Membership increased during the 1830s and 1840s, but arguments split the movement into different factions. Not all were committed to the social equality of blacks, and some objected to their very presence, indicating that race was a salient issue in the North as well. Nevertheless, attacking slavery was the priority, and every opportunity was exploited to force public opinion upon the issue. Initially highly unpopular—violent mobs routinely broke up abolitionist meetings, and in 1837 Elijah Lovejoy, publisher of an anti-slavery newspaper, was murdered in Alton, Illinois—the message gained more support within Northern society by the 1850s. Garrison's immediatism, seen as excessive by many, was toned down by others into a more mainstream anti-slavery stance that did not stipulate black equality or even abolition in the South, but was concerned to keep slavery out of new territory in the West.

The South, however, did not distinguish between these positions. Any attack upon slavery was regarded as a fundamental affront to the whole Southern way of life, and a siege mentality developed. During the 1850s, a series of bitter

> "Mine was as the taper light; His was the burning sun. I could live for the slave: John Brown could *die* for him." *Frederick Douglass,* on John Brown

political confrontations boiled down to one issue: what was slavery's future in the nation? Material and idealistic differences between the North and South had become so great that perhaps two disparate civilizations existed within the United States by 1860.

Industrialization was well under way in the North. A working-class population concentrated in great cities, such as Boston, New York, and Philadelphia, included both native-born Americans and immigrants. They worked for wages,

The Washington Artillery of New Orleans. Their commitment and enthusiasm almost made up for their lack of modern equipment and consistent support.

were highly mobile, and believed in the superiority of free labor as the market revolution changed the character of Northern society. A dynamic culture sprang up that stressed individuality, education, and reform. Technological advances enabled an increasingly literate public to read cheap novels and newspapers. Recreational activities became more important as the divide between "home" and "work" was established.

The South, by contrast, retained an agrarian economy and culture that seemed to have changed very little since the Revolution. Slavery tended to hinder industrial development as profits were plowed not into new industrial or agricultural method but back into buying more land and slaves. Urbanization was similarly stunted, and by 1860, the South had just five cities with 50,000 inhabitants. Most white Southerners seemed to prefer it that way; they did not want factories and urban squalor in their midst. Poverty, social conflict, and the impersonality of materialism contrasted with a stable, hierarchical Southern society characterized by honor, family, and independence.

It would be easy to exaggerate the differences between North and South, and historians have noted common features. However, regional trends pointed to substantial divergence between the North and South, with slavery as the fundamental cause. Abolitionist and proslavery advocates greatly influenced public and political opinion, making further compromise impossible by the late 1850s. They had helped to create a sectional mentality that divided the Union into North and South in the minds of Americans.

Thus, whether the two societies were dramatically different or essentially sim-

Meanwhile, in the North, industry turned out thousands of cannons, millions of shells, and all the material a modern army would need to sustain its objectives.

ilar did not really matter. What counted was that millions of ordinary Americans perceived themselves to be Northerners or Southerners, placing a sectional loyalty above that of the Union. Once that point had been reached, armed conflict seemed inevitable.

Two important issues were resolved by the Civil War. First, the fragile basis of the nation was finally stregthened. With rapid territorial expansion, unprecedented immigration, clear ethnic and religious differences, not to mention the sectional divide, many Europeans had not expected the United States to survive. Confederate general Robert E. Lee's surrender confirmed the political unity of both North and South under one flag. Never again would such a challenge to the very fabric of American society be made. Second, slavery was abolished and four million African Americans became U.S. citizens. Although subsequent developments would question the quality of their freedom, this should not alter the significance of slavery's demise. Certainly, no matter how bad life became for black Southerners, they did not underestimate the importance of President Lincoln's Emancipation Proclamation, January 1, 1863.

Lincoln's party, stunned by his assassination on April 14, 1865, attempted to rebuild the South. They faced a daunting task. If reeling from the economic and human cost of the Civil War and the humiliation of defeat were not bad enough, the very foundation of Southern society had crumbled with emancipation. Republicans tried to implement equality in a social order conditioned by centuries of slavery. Although legal measures could be passed, deeply ingrained attitudes proved impossible to change. The problem was exacerbated by an appalling economic situation in which a return to cotton proved fatal to long-term recovery and created antagonism between sharecroppers —farmers who handed the landowner a share of the year's crop as a form of rent—and employers. However, given the success of cotton in the antebellum period, its replanting was entirely logical.

Nagging doubts about black equality in the North, which developed into race riots during the 1860s as an influx of freedmen was expected, ultimately doomed the success of Reconstruction. A minority of Radical Republicans believed in integration, but most of their constituents shared similar prejudices toward blacks as did the South. Indeed, free blacks in the North were barred from voting and subject to discriminatory laws in most states.

Thus, initial public euphoria and sympathy for the slave, augmented by the contribution made by black military regiments in the Civil War, waned as Reconstruction dragged on. People tired of the "Southern question" preferred to leave the region to govern itself. The North capitulated to Southern desires for home rule by 1877, allowing the South to implement segregation laws (known as Jim Crow), and stood by as African Americans were lynched in the name of white supremacy.

The African-American response to segregation in the late nineteenth century was severely constrained by a climate of racial violence and bigotry. On one level, the black community seemed to accept the new laws. Booker T. Washington (1856–1915), a former slave who had become the most famous African American by the turn of the century, exemplified and indeed formulated this response. Washington built a powerful organization, known as the "Tuskegee Machine," which controlled black newspapers and organizations across the South and extended into the North. His Atlanta Compromise address, given in 1895, set up a doctrine of accommodation that, although not supporting political and social inequality, accepted Jim Crow, at least until blacks had overcome the debilitating effects of slavery.

Booker T. Washington voiced a common belief that bondage had retarded the development of African Americans as a race, a problem he felt could only be tackled by a program of industrial education that taught basic trade skills. He told his white audience in Atlanta that "ignorant and inexperienced . . . we began at the top instead of at the bottom." A new economic partnership between the races could revive the South's future, Washington argued. As his white audience wondered what the implications might be, he assuaged their fears by saying "in all things that are purely social we can be as separate as

"We have devoured the land and our animals eat up the wheat and cornfields close. All the people retire before us and desolation is behind. To realize what war is, one should follow our tracks."
General William T. Sherman, 1864

the fingers, yet one as the hand in all things essential to mutual progress."

The Atlanta Compromise address won universal approval throughout white America, but Northern black critics accused Washington of selling out to white racists. However, his position was less clear-cut than it might have seemed. His educational and industrial initiatives were dependent upon finance from white benefactors attracted by his conciliatory message. In public, he stressed accommodation and compliance, but privately he spoke of resistance and justice. Washington funded a number of legal challenges to Jim Crow and wrote unsigned newspaper editorials protesting against segregation. His example

The South suffered massive destruction during the course of the war. As early as 1861, Richmond, as shown in this photograph, had experienced bombardment and fire.

challenged notions of inferiority during an era when racism was pervasive in both North and South.

Moreover, Washington appreciated that the black community did not necessarily want widespread integration. African-American businesses developed upon the needs of an exclusively black clientele as the separation between the races was enforced. "Separate but equal" did not bring equal facilities, but it did at least require that some facilities be built for African Americans. This was a progression from the days when blacks were simply excluded from schools, hospitals, and many other areas of Southern life. Given the vigorous resistance by many whites to any change, evidenced by the horrific increase in lynchings, Washington felt constrained in developing an appropriate strategy.

Segregation laws drove a barrier between blacks and whites that would not be broken until the Civil Rights movement in the 1950s and 1960s. However, the realities of Southern life did not discriminate between races, as economic hardship and poverty faced most families. As the region adjusted to emancipation, slavery cast a shadow over attempts to create a New South.

SLAVERY AND THE SOUTH

> "There can be
> no moral right
> in the enslaving
> of one man by
> another."
> *Abraham
> Lincoln*

The proclamation by the Declaration of Independence that "all men are created equal" put the problem of slavery in American society into sharper focus. In the northern and middle states, emancipation acts curtailed slavery between 1774 and 1804, leaving the South—states below the Mason-Dixon line—as the sole domain of the "peculiar institution," as slavery was called. Far from dying out as some had hoped, slavery flourished in the antebellum South. In simple economic terms, slavery was highly profitable. Cotton, the main export crop, required intensive labor and commanded high prices in newly industrialized countries like Great Britain, where textiles were a key industry. Between 1800 and 1860, cotton accounted for approximately half of the nation's total exports, boosting the Northern economy as well as being the basis of Southern economic life. Slavery grew rapidly and moved westward and southward as the United States expanded across the continent. Large numbers of slaves moved out of Virginia and the Carolinas into new states and territories such as Alabama, Mississippi, and Louisiana. Nevertheless, the census of 1860 recorded that there were just 385,000 slaveowners out of approximately 1,500,000 white families (the total white population being eight million), with only a small percentage being of planter status (twenty slaves or more).

The South developed a dual economy. A large percentage of non-slaveholding whites lived in up-country areas, away from the Black Belt (the region's most fertile soil), in semisubsistence farming and herding communities with independent traditions. Other whites aspired to slaveholding status, which rather than being a fixed social class was a fluid category that people moved in and out of.

Slavery proved to be highly flexible. Sugar, rice, and indigo plantations were found in the swampy coastal areas of South Carolina, Georgia, and Louisiana. Other staple crops, corn, maize, and wheat, were grown on almost all farms. Corn fitted in with the growing season of cotton so conveniently that it was the South's most cultivated crop. Slaves were also found in urban areas and industrial factories, although the South remained predominantly a rural, agricultural society.

The human cost of slavery has been far more difficult to calculate. Most historians would stress the slaves' enduring capacity to carve out a rich and supportive cultural environment, but recently there has been an equal emphasis placed upon the brutal nature of the slave system. Most distressing for slaves was the forced severing of families and communities by the internal slave trade. Punishment was routinely administered and there was little defense against the rape of female slaves by owners. An immense physical and psychological strain must have weighed heavily upon slaves yearning for freedom for themselves, their partners, and their children. However, the fact that there was a self-reproducing slave population, in contrast to other New World slave societies, indicated the success of the African-American slave community. Between 1800 and 1860, the slave population went from approximately 900,000 to four million. Founded upon a supportive and distinctive blend of Christianity and African religion, folklore, and conjurism, slave communities achieved a measure of cultural autonomy that served to distance them from the otherwise pervasive control of slaveholders.

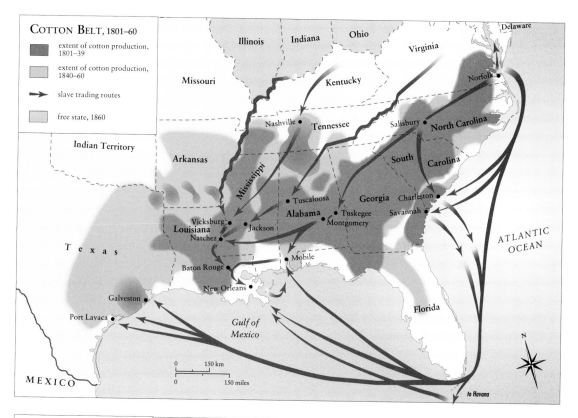

COTTON BELT, 1801–60

extent of cotton production, 1801–39

extent of cotton production, 1840–60

→ slave trading routes

free state, 1860

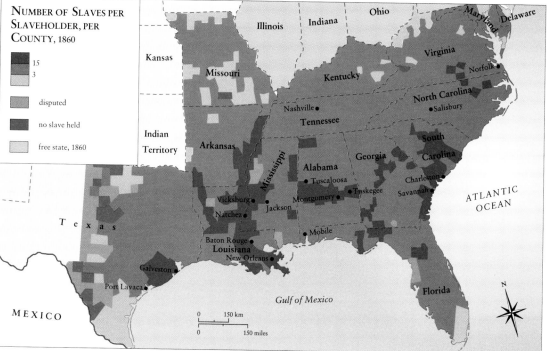

NUMBER OF SLAVES PER SLAVEHOLDER, PER COUNTY, 1860

15
3

disputed

no slave held

free state, 1860

ORIGINS OF THE CIVIL WAR

When Abraham Lincoln said that "a house divided against itself cannot stand," he expressed a widespread feeling within the United States that slavery and freedom could not coexist. The problem of slavery was so great that it had been placed beyond the limits of discussion in the antebellum period, but by 1860, that no longer seemed possible. Thus, although numerous factors have been cited, most historians would agree that slavery was the root cause of the Civil War.

Westward expansion, upon which the success of the country rested, was also the major cause of tension between the slave and free states. This paradox holds the key to understanding why, in 1860, compromise could no longer be maintained. As new territory was acquired, Congress had to decide how it would be incorporated into the Union. Politicians tried to maintain a balance between North and South, as southerners realized that the industrial superiority and a rapidly expanding population gave the North more seats in Congress.

The Missouri Compromise of 1820 seemed to have solved the problem by fixing the boundary between slave and free states at the line of 36° 30′, with the new slave state of Missouri being north of that latitude. However, the gains from the Mexican War reopened the debate between 1846 and 1850, as Northern congressmen supported the Wilmot Proviso to keep slavery out of the Southwest. Only a unanimous rejection by Southern senators prevented the passage of the Wilmot Proviso, which must have emphasized just how precarious the situation was becoming; fifteen free states and fifteen slave states kept a balance of power, allowing the South a veto. Any change in that situation, though, would disrupt the status quo. In a highly charged atmosphere, the great statesman Henry Clay proposed a number of new compromises, collectively known as the Compromise of 1850, which placated both sides, at least for a time.

A succession of incidents in the 1850s saw sectional tension escalate to critical levels. Northern reaction to the 1850 compromise was hostile, as a number of abolitionists and politicians openly proclaimed their defiance of the Fugitive Slave Law (requiring the return of escaped slaves by free states), which infuriated the South. The Kansas-Nebraska Act, attempting to limit the geographical expansion of slavery, passed in May 1854, prompted a bitter

When the Democratic party split into Northern and Southern halves, Abraham Lincoln won the presidential election. He took office on March 4, 1861. Meanwhile in Montgomery, Alabama, delegates from seven southern states had met and provisionally formed the Confederate States of America.

struggle between pro- and anti-slavery supporters over the organization of the vast territory west of Missouri and Iowa. The Whigs found it impossible to maintain a unity of Northern and Southern interests, leading to the collapse of the second party system. In their place emerged the Republican Party, composed of a number of different groups, but generally committed to a free soil policy (which meant keeping slavery out of any new territory). The Supreme Court's decision in the Dred Scott case (1857)—holding that a slave taken into free state remained a slave, since citizenship is defined by states—also stirred up matters, encouraging Southerners to think that slavery could not be banned from the West. John Brown's raid at Harpers Ferry on October 16, 1859, which tried to initiate a full-scale slave revolt in the South, dramatically exemplified a decade that had split the nation into two sections. Abraham Lincoln's presidential victory in 1860 solidified the divide between North and South.

PRESIDENTIAL
ELECTION, 1860

- Lincoln (Republican)
- Douglas (Democrat)
- Breckinridge (Democrat)
- Bell (Constitutional Union)
- no returns
- divided commitments
- – – Missouri Compromise line, 1820

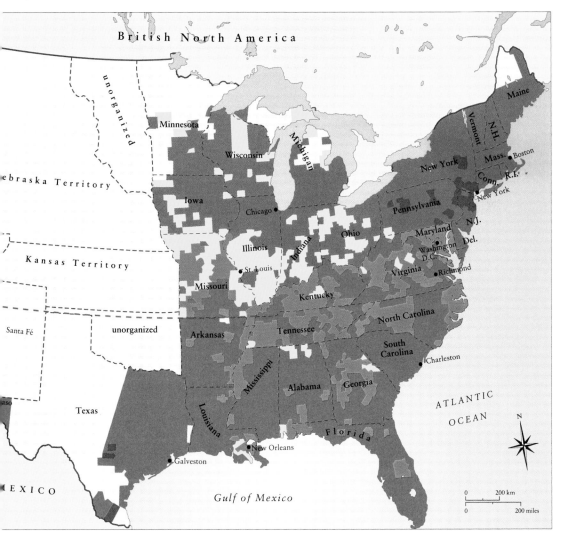

CIVIL WAR—OPENING MOVES

The election of Abraham Lincoln to the Presidency on November 6, 1860, fixed the route to secession of Southern states. With less than 40 percent of the popular vote going to Lincoln, and with four candidates sharing the electoral college vote, Lincoln could not claim a strong national mandate. Nonetheless, when South Carolina seceded on December 20, followed by ten more states until Tennessee became the last state to join the rebellion on June 8, 1861, Lincoln chose to make preservation of the Union his justification for raising an army, stressing national unity rather than political division. The Confederate States of America formed a government and elected Jefferson Davis as president during meetings in Montgomery, Alabama, in February 1860; they declared Richmond, Virginia, their capital by May 1860, but as far as Lincoln was concerned this was a Southern "insurrection."

The North had a huge population and resource advantage over the South. The population was four times as large as the free population of the Confederate states. Manufacturing industry, communications infrastructure, banking facilities, and even food production were all concentrated in the Union states. The South had its cotton, but with European nations choosing neutrality, and the Northern navy blockading Southern ports, profitable trade was severely limited. North of the border in Canada, industry prospered from military orders to supply Union armies. Even so, the South was hopeful that the North would tire of the effort needed to reclaim the seceded states. The South had only to hold its borders for victory. The North would have to invade and conquer. The Confederacy might win this kind of confrontation even with a resource disadvantage.

Early engagements gave Southern leaders some cause for hope. One resource that the North lacked was military leadership in the field. The aging General Winfield Scott was perceptive in analysis, but not up to the demands of this conflict, and Generals McClellan, Burnside, and Hooker, among others, proved faulty. In the South, J.E.B. Stuart, Robert E. Lee, Thomas "Stonewall" Jackson, and their colleagues provided skilled and powerful leadership.

In April 1861, the small federal garrison in Fort Sumter, Charleston, surrendered to South Carolina troops after having been trapped without new provisions for months, but major direct confrontations did not come immediately. The western counties of Virginia broke away to form a Unionist government, and early Northern victories such as that in Phillippi, Virginia, helped protect this strategically important area. However, in the first major confrontation,

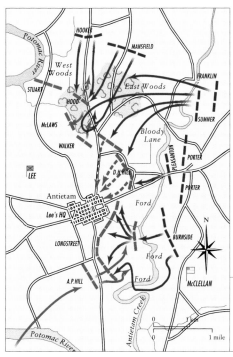

ANTIETAM, SEPTEMBER 17, 1862

- — Confederate forces
- — Union forces
- army commanders
- → Union advance
- → Confederate advance
- ⇢ Confederate retreat

the close-fought First Battle of Bull Run (Manassas, Virginia; July 21, 1861), the "stonewalling" tactics that gave Jackson his nickname contributed to a victory that inspired Southern hopes and undermined the Northern belief that this would be a brief campaign. Union defeats at Wilson's Creek, Missouri (August 10, 1861), and Ball's Bluff, Virginia (October 21, 1861), lowered Northern morale.

There were Union victories. Grant took Forts Henry and Donelson in Tennessee (February 1862), provoking the Confederate evacuation of Nashville. At the Battle of Shiloh (Pittsburg Landing, Tennessee; April 6–7, 1862), Grant defended successfully against a Confederate attack, but over 20,000 casualties signaled the toll that this war would take. Fort Pulaski, Georgia, fell to the Union on April 11. Two weeks later, Union admiral Farragut occupied New Orleans.

Meanwhile, Stonewall Jackson, with a relatively small force, tied up Union manpower with a vigorous and mobile campaign of attrition in the Shenandoah Valley. In the east, General McClellan simultaneously launched the Peninsula Campaign, which aimed to take the Confederate capital of Richmond. With strategy and caution that frustrated his Northern master, McClellan advanced tentatively, halted some twenty miles from Richmond, and after almost three months in the field was pushed back by Robert E. Lee to Harrison's Landing, Virginia (July 2, 1862), ending for a time the North's ambition on Richmond.

Victories for Jackson at Cedar Mountain, Virginia (August 9, 1862), and for the Southern generals at the Second Battle of Bull Run (August 30, 1862), together with Jackson's forces taking the strategically significant Harpers Ferry, West Virginia (September 15, 1862), appeared to put the South into a strong position.

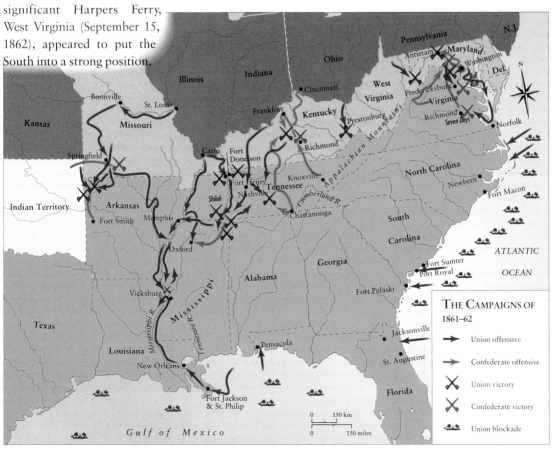

THE CAMPAIGNS OF 1861–62

→ Union offensive

→ Confederate offensive

✕ Union victory

✕ Confederate victory

⚓ Union blockade

71

CIVIL WAR—TOTAL WAR

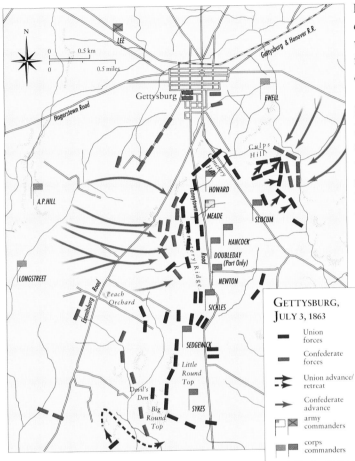

Gettysburg & Hanover R.R.

Hagerstown Road

N

0   0.5 km

0   0.5 miles

Gettysburg

LEE

EWELL

Culps Hill

HOWARD

Smoky

Taneytown Road

MEADE

SLOCUM

HANCOCK

A.P.HILL

DOUBLEDAY
(Part Only)

LONGSTREET

NEWTON

Emmitsburg Road

Peach Orchard

SICKLES

SEDGEWICK

Cemetery Ridge

Little Round Top

Devil's Den

Big Round Top

SYKES

GETTYSBURG, JULY 3, 1863

- Union forces
- Confederate forces
- Union advance/ retreat
- Confederate advance
- army commanders
- corps commanders

Even at the height of Southern success, the fragility of that authority was evident. Fighting the war on all fronts was draining the Confederacy of resources.

The armies that met at the battle of Antietam (Sharpsburg, Maryland) on September 17, 1862, numbered over 100,000 men in total, with the Union side having an advantage of about two to one. The Northern troops benefited from their superior manpower and weaponry, and caused immense damage to the Confederates. Lee's army might have been destroyed, but the Northern army, led by McClellan, worried that unexpected Southern reinforcements might arrive and failed to press home their advantage. There were over 23,000 casualties, still the highest American loss of life on any one day of any war. Lee's Confederate army had been fought to a standstill, and the pool of Confederate soldiers was becoming dangerously depleted. In Washington, D.C., Lincoln published the Emancipation Proclamation, declaring from January 1, 1863, the freedom of all slaves in any state or district still in rebellion. Liberating slaves over whom the Union now had power might seem futile, but it acknowledged at last that slavery was a central issue of the war, and it set in motion the inevitable journey to the Thirteenth Amendment, declaring slavery unconstitutional.

The South was by no means defeated. Lee routed the forces of Union General Burnside at Fredericksburg, Virginia (December 13, 1862), and at Stones River (Murfreesboro, Tennessee; January 2, 1863), the Union advance on Chattanooga was checked. But each battle brought thousands more casualties. In May 1863, General Lee engineered a major Southern victory against General Hooker's Northern forces at Chancellorsville. Among the 13,000 Confederate casualties was Stonewall Jackson, dead after being accidentally shot by a Southern guard. When Lee crossed the Potomac in late June, heading for Pennsylvania, the disorganized Union Army seemed unready for the challenge, but the Battle of Gettysburg (July 1–3, 1863) was a massive defeat for the South, and the two sides suffered total casualties exceeding 50,000.

Grant spent 1863 driving a wedge through the South by gaining control of the Mississippi. A series of victories culminated in the surrender of Vicksburg (July 4, 1863). A Union defeat at Chickamauga, Georgia (September 19–20, 1863), caused 34,000 casualties, more than half suffered by the Southern forces. The Union retreat to Chattanooga was followed by a hard-driving advance by Grant that drove the Confederate forces out of the field.

In 1864, General Sherman took advantage of the Union's controlling positions to drive through the south to Savannah and the sea, inflicting immense damage on Atlanta (September 2, 1863). His military journey, known as Sherman's March, took him through Georgia in late 1864, and then into the Carolinas in early 1865. He occupied Charleston on February 17, 1865, and was victorious at Bentonville, North Carolina, on March 19–20.

Starting his move toward Richmond, Grant was fought to a temporary standstill at Spotsylvania, Virginia (May 8–12, 1864), but each battle cost the South casualties that it could not afford, and weakened the capacity for resistance. On November 30, 1864, the defeat of Confederate General Hood at Chattanooga effectively rid the Union of any threat in that region. When Grant defeated Lee's forces at Fort Steadman, Virginia (March 25, 1865), the days of the Confederacy were effectively over. Union troops entered Richmond on April 3, 1865, after the Confederate army and government had left the city. Five days later, Robert E. Lee surrendered to Ulysses S. Grant at Appomattox Court House. Over 600,000 had died, almost twice as many from the North as from the South. In Canada there were fears that the Union army, almost one million strong, may march north as a consequence of British support for the Confederate government. However, this threat did not materialize, as the U.S. government had more pressing demands on its resources.

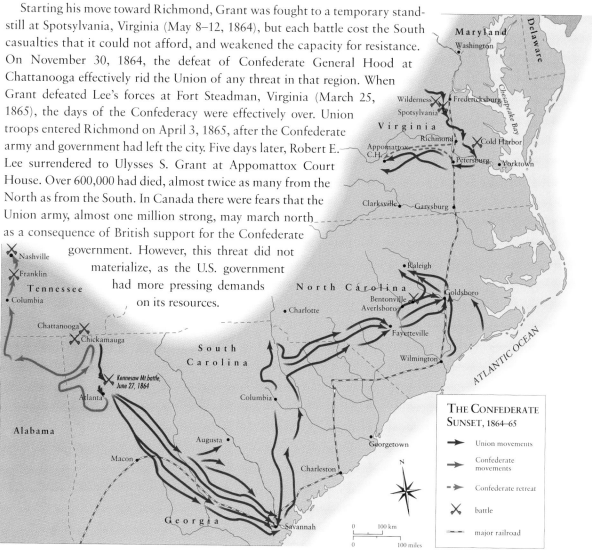

THE CONFEDERATE
SUNSET, 1864–65

→ Union movements

→ Confederate movements

-→ Confederate retreat

✕ battle

--- major railroad

RECONSTRUCTION

The cartoonist Thomas Nast, a radical Republican sympathizer, attacks the Reconstruction policies of President Johnson, using a Shakespearian theme; Johnson as Iago poisons the mind of Othello (shown here as a Union veteran).

During Reconstruction, 1865–1877, the South was occupied by Northern troops in five military districts as terms of readmission to the Union were debated. These twelve years saw a flurry of activity as complex maneuvers in Washington affected all aspects of Southern life. The period can be viewed from political, social, and economic perspectives.

Reconstruction entailed an unprecedented amount of new legislation. Three amendments were made to the U.S. Constitution and a number of other bills passed to establish equal rights for African Americans, mostly after the Republican Party had won a large majority in Congress from January 1867. With good reason this period is known as Radical Reconstruction. These measures were taken in response to President Andrew Johnson's perceived leniency (as former Confederates received title to their confiscated and abandoned land) and to Southern refusal to change. State governments in the South had demonstrated their intransigence by passing Black Codes in 1865 and 1866, which, although acknowledging the end of slavery, severely restricted the rights of blacks. Bitter debates in Congress, which led to the impeachment of Johnson in 1868, were common, emphasizing the controversial nature of the legislation. By 1877, in legal terms at least, African Americans were full citizens of the United States.

State government in the South was also dramatically affected. By 1870, all former Confederate states had been readmitted, as new Republican Party administrations were formed. Three groups were involved. "Carpetbaggers" were northerners who had come to the South in order to remold the region upon principles of free labor. "Scalawags" were native Southerners who in general had a positive attitude toward change, including Unionists, nonslaveholding whites, and even some planters. Finally, from the ranks of the freedmen came leaders who had formerly been free blacks, slave ministers, or veterans of the war. African Americans composed the electoral majority in some Southern states and were voted into office for the first time, although never in proportion to their numbers. Many conflicting motives explained the emergence of these new political groups, including the desire of some to profit from the situation, but despite much mythmaking the record of state administrations was generally sound. They reformed taxes and the local judiciary system, built more schools and hospitals, outlawed discrimination, and embarked upon economic redevelopment.

Travel was unrestricted, and reunited African-American families got used to the autonomy that freedom brought. Despite increased political participation,

REESTABLISHMENT OF CONSERVATIVE GOVERNMENTS, 1869–77

1870 year of readmission of state in the Union

1873 year of reestablishment of conservative government

reestablished 1869–71

reestablished 1873–74

reestablished 1876–77

military district

Map labels:
Virginia *1870* 1869
Tennessee *1866* 1869
North Carolina *1868* 1870
Arkansas *1868* 1874
Mississippi
South Carolina *1868* 1876
Alabama *1868* 1874
Georgia *1870* 1871
Texas *1870* 1873
Louisiana *1868* 1877
Florida *1868* 1877

0 400 km
0 400 miles

blacks withdrew from white society in social terms. This trend was most apparent in the religious structure of the South, which, though white-led, had seen biracial congregations in the antebellum period. The black community developed a network of church affiliations that provided mutual support and aid in what was an uncertain situation. That uncertainty was accentuated by whites who refused to accept racial equality. The Ku Klux Klan, formed in Tennessee in 1866, was the most famous of a number of white supremacist organizations dedicated to the restoration of the racial status quo. Slavery's legacy—racism—was not all-pervasive among whites, but in the hands of propagandists and a worsening economic situation, blacks became a convenient target.

Economic policy is generally considered Reconstruction's greatest failure, in particular regarding access to land. After the Civil War, freedmen expected to cash in on Washington's promise of "forty acres and a mule," a process begun by General Sherman and continued for a short time by the Freedmen's Bureau, their hopes resting upon land ownership as the best means of self-sufficiency. However, property rights had long been protected by law, and the redistribution of land was not acceptable to most white Americans. The Freedmen's Bureau, set up in March 1865, provided food and medical supplies, had educational responsibilities, and advised on wage contracts, but was no longer allowed to redistribute confiscated land, despite the wishes of some politicians and Bureau commissioners. Thus, Reconstruction saw a struggle between former planters and slaves to define the terms of a new labor system, which continued long after the last Northern troops had left in 1877. At stake was the very meaning and character of freedom.

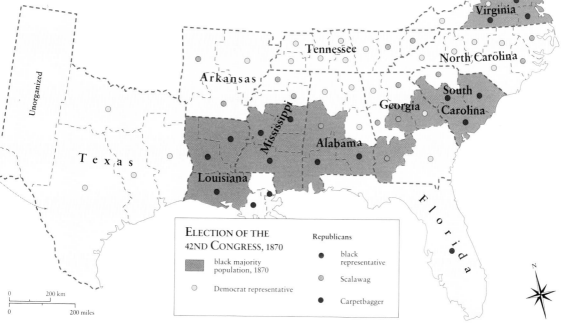

ELECTION OF THE
42ND CONGRESS, 1870

black majority
population, 1870

Democrat representative

Republicans

● black
representative

○ Scalawag

● Carpetbagger

THE NEW SOUTH

A sharecropper plows his rented land, paying for the use of the land and probably the animals and implememts by giving the owner about half of the crop grown.

Severe economic problems hampered Southern recovery. Old habits died hard as the South returned to the widespread production of cotton. The plantation system had broken up, but with the failure of land redistribution, the best acreage remained in the hands of the few. Freedmen looking for independence were thus forced to rent land from their former owners, which was difficult given the chronic shortage of money within the South. To overcome this problem, a complex and widely variable agreement evolved between owners and those who wanted to work their land.

Two arrangements were common. Sharecroppers "paid" for land, accommodation, and supplies by promising a share of their crop, usually about half. Tenant farmers were in a slightly more advantageous position, often owning their own tools and maybe a mule, and kept a larger share of the harvest, commonly three-fourths of the cash crop (cotton) and two-thirds of the subsistence crop (corn). However, the tenant farmer was forced to mortgage the fruits of his labor further to get supplies at the local store—an arrangement known as the crop lien.

This new labor system tended to leave tenants and sharecoppers in a vulnerable position. If the crop failed, or the price of cotton fluctuated (and the price per bale fell from about thirty cents in the 1860s to just ten cents in the 1880s), farmers were left with unpaid bills. A cycle of debt developed that became impossible to break, restricting mobility and autonomy. A depression in 1873 exacerbated a still war-torn economy, forcing many formerly independent white farmers into sharecropping, a pattern often repeated in the New South.

Thus a ruralized labor force of black and white sharecroppers developed, manipulated by landlords and merchants. This small elite was composed of former planters and a new merchant class, who were themselves subject to the financial control of Northern business interests.

In the face of this worsening situation, a number of journalists and politicians, led by Henry Grady, the editor of the *Atlanta Constitution*, began to plan a "new"

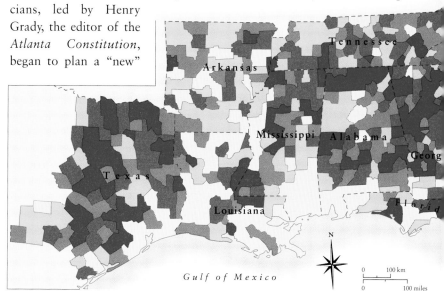

South in the 1880s. The basic message was one of diversification and industrialization that powerfully captured the popular imagination. Tax exemptions were offered to businesses relocating to the South, and cheap convict labor was also made available. The South expanded its railtrack mileage considerably, bringing previously isolated regions into the market economy as goods came within reach of commercial markets. Between 1880 and 1900, the number of cotton mills increased from 161 to 400, and many more tobacco factories were built. Other industries followed. Located in the center of a region rich in iron ore, coal, and limestone deposits, the city of Birmingham, Alabama, developed a thriving industrial economy. The roar of blast furnaces and railroad yards characterized the city. Chattanooga, Tennessee, was also a powerhouse of industrial production, possessssing seventeen furnaces, nine foundries, and a number of machine shops.

However, despite some success, accompanied by a lot of publicity, the reality of economic development was somewhat different. Industry in the South was on a small-scale, semiskilled basis. By 1900, the South had just 10 percent of the nation's factories, a smaller percentage than in 1860, and just 15 percent of Southerners were engaged in manufacturing. Urban growth, the basis of modern society, lagged far behind the North. The nostalgic myth of the Lost Cause—a romantic hankering to the days of the Old South—epitomized a South in which industry may have taken root, but not the values of industrialization.

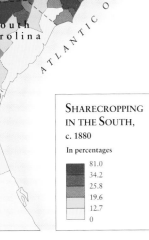

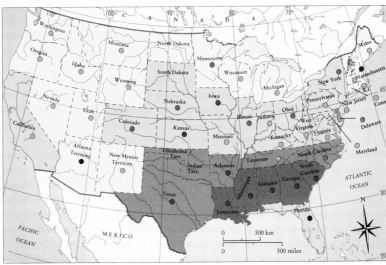

SHARECROPPING IN THE SOUTH, c. 1880

In percentages

81.0
34.2
25.8
19.6
12.7
0

COTTON PRICES, 1870 – 1900

price per pound in cents

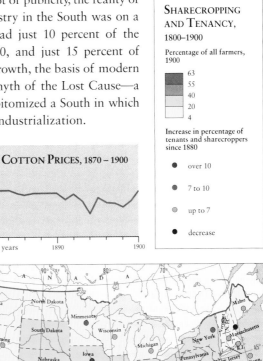

SHARECROPPING AND TENANCY, 1800–1900

Percentage of all farmers, 1900

63
55
40
20
4

Increase in percentage of tenants and sharecroppers since 1880

● over 10

● 7 to 10

● up to 7

● decrease

JIM CROW—THE RISE OF SEGREGATION

Jim Crow was a famous character in minstrel shows whose name came to represent the system of racial segregation that arose in the South in the late nineteenth and early twentieth centuries. Segregation provided a short term solution to the question of race relations in the South, which had been in flux since the abolition of slavery.

There have been many arguments over whether legal segregation simply codified social practice. Certainly, blacks and whites had begun to withdraw into their own communities during Reconstruction. It seems likely that the challenge of the Populist Party, which for the first time in decades threatened Democratic majorities in Southern states, was the catalyst for a concerted legislative effort to disenfranchise African Americans.

This policy was first seen in the drafting of new state constitutions in the 1890s. At a convention in 1890, Mississippi barred criminals from voting and imposed a $2 poll tax. Voting also required the ability to read the Constitution, or at least be able to understand it. The interpretation of this law was left to polling officials, who used it to blatantly discriminate against black voters. The estimated impact was to disenfranchise 123,000 blacks and just 11,000 whites. South Carolina followed Mississippi in 1895, under the leadership of Ben Tillman, who was so keen to implement these changes that he returned from the Senate to serve as chairman of the Committee on the Rights of Suffrage. In 1898, Louisiana added the "grandfather clause" to the other discriminatory devices, which granted suffrage to all males whose fathers or grandfathers had been qualified to vote on January 1, 1867, a date when blacks were not registered.

Other states followed suit. By 1910, African Americans had been disenfranchised in Alabama, Georgia, North Carolina, Oklahoma, and Virginia. A series of laws ensured the complete separation of the races in public spaces. Some had been passed in the 1880s, but the vast majority came between 1898 and 1915. Jim Crow legislation covered transport, schools, hospitals, parks, restaurants, courts, hotels, cemeteries, and even washrooms.

The Supreme Court upheld the actions of Southern state governments in *Plessy v. Ferguson*. Homer Plessy challenged a Louisiana law that segregated rail carriages on racial grounds by mandating "equal but separate accommodations for the white and colored races." Plessy, one-eighth black, was arrested in 1892 after refusing to ride in the Jim Crow carriage, resulting in a lawsuit that progressed to the Supreme Court in 1896. Plessy objected that his right to equal protection of the laws established by the Thirteenth and Fourteenth Amendments had been violated, but the Court upheld the constitutionality of the Louisiana law by a majority of seven to one. Despite the opposition of Justice John Marshall Harlan, who said that the Constitution was "color-blind," the Court's verdict established the doctrine of "separate but equal" upon which the South justified its system.

Legal segregation was buttressed by racial violence. The New South saw a rise in lynchings in the 1880s and 1890s, which continued into the first decades of the twentieth century. Violence against African Americans was a ritualized form of terror, which often involved whole communities, and seemed to arise out of the psychological fears of whites.

This political cartoon attacks organizations such as the White League and the Ku Klux Klan for promoting racial attacks on the freed slaves in the South, particularly denying access to the ballot box and education.

EDUCATION AND SEGREGATION

States without compulsory school attendance

1880   1900

states practicing discriminatory voting laws, with date of legislation

PART IV: SPANNING THE CONTINENT

A resident of Chicago who emerged from a fifty-year sleep in 1920 would hardly believe his observations. Elevated railways ran through the city center. Horseless carriages (automobiles) proceeded along wide avenues where horse-drawn wagons had traveled. The incessant noise of construction crews working on buildings that stretched to the sky seemed inescapable. Throngs of shoppers entered and exited stores whose large windows displayed an array of goods that appeared to have no obvious function. This time-traveler would awake to a different world—marked by new forms of transportation, innovative construction techniques, novel ways of marketing goods, and an environment capable of accommodating a more diverse and larger population. The city had become the crossroads of North America. Its rail hub received and dispatched goods across the continent. Its industries thrived. Its success drew migrants from within and outside the continent of North America to share in this expansion.

In this poster from 1882, the Illinois Central Railroad advertises its services. By 1893 six major railroad companies had completed lines connecting the East to the western seaboard.

Indeed, Chicago represented a microcosm of the dramatic changes in society. There, industrial workshops manufactured goods for customers near and far. Corporations, with branches in outlying areas within the United States and overseas, established headquarters there. Generators, providing electricity for telephone communication, factory production, and a myriad of household appliances, were based there. Immigrant communities developed there, the city serving as an incubator for the making of new Americans. As the United States and Canada industrialized, they became more urban; growing cities were a focus of capital investment in expanding commercial enterprises, many with large numbers of workers producing consumer goods connected to national systems of transportation and distribution, which in turn continued to fuel the expansion of cities. In brief, industrialization and urbanization were interdependent processes.

Chicago provides a powerful example of this symbiotic relationship. The "Windy City," already a railway hub and industrial center, was home to 300,000 people in 1870. In subsequent decades, it developed impressively and became the nation's second-largest city in 1920, with a population of 2.7 million. Throughout this period, Chicago served as a "gateway to the West," linking the producers of raw materials with the manufacturers of finished goods. Cattle from Wyoming made it to the killing floors of Armour and Swift slaughterhouses; iron ore found its way to the South Side steel plants; and wheat from U.S. and Canadian prairies traveled by rail to the city's mills, where it was processed into flour. Chicago was home to International Harvester, manufacturer of over 80 percent of the North American market for agricultural machinery, including combine harvesters, which significantly increased farmers' productivity and lowered their production costs. Hart, Schaffner and Marx helped make Chicago the second-largest manufacturer of ready-made clothing. Pullman, a suburb of Chicago, produced the passenger car equipped with sleeping facilities that was carried by virtually every railway in the United States.

Such economic activity required a steady supply of labor, increasingly provided by immigrants, mainly from Europe. Steel mills employed Eastern European immigrants to work at blast furnaces, where they were supervised by the sons of Irish immigrants. Polish immigrants settled for the most dangerous and lower-paid jobs in the meatpacking industry, and after 1915 were joined by African Americans, who participated in the "great migration" from the rural South to the urban North. Jewish immigrant men and women from czarist Russia gravitated to New York's and Chicago's garment trades, whose manufacturers and contractors were predominantly descendants of German-Jewish or Austrian-Hungarian immigrants.

The integration of those from rural, agricultural backgrounds, or otherwise unfamiliar with industrial work, into wage labor signified that as the American working class developed, it became more multiethnic and multiracial in its composition. To be sure, not every immigrant was a manual worker, nor every manual worker an immigrant; but since almost half of the population of such industrial centers as New York, Chicago, Pittsburgh, and Cleveland were foreign-born at the turn of the century, it is safe to conclude that the immigrant experience was inextricably bound to the expansion of wage labor.

Class formation can be understood in the context of shifts in economic organization, production systems, and labor markets—all of which influenced the development of cities. Of primary importance is the transition from entrepreneurial capitalism to corporate capitalism, in which the center of power moved from individual proprietors to a board of directors who shared the rights of ownership with other stockholders and shared control of the firm with managers who oversaw its day-to-day operations.

"The growth of a large business is merely the survival of the fittest. . . . The American Beauty rose can be produced in the splendor and fragrance which bring cheer to its beholder only by sacrificing the early buds which grow up around it."
John D. Rockefeller,
1902

The growing ascendancy of the corporation represented challenges and opportunities presented by the expansion of large-scale enterprise. Chicago's meatpacking houses employed on the average less than 100 workers in 1870 but over 1,100 in 1920. U.S. Steel in 1903 consisted of 200 subsidiary companies, employing some 168,000 workers in Pennsylvania, Ohio, Indiana, and Illinois.

Chicago in the 1920s. Crowds pass by the Mandel Brothers store on the corner of Madison and State Streets, said to be the busiest corner in the world.

In the interest of efficiency these businesses developed a structure and modus operandi that stressed the functional autonomy of subsidiaries, branches, divisions, and departments, as well as the coordination of activities for which each was responsible. Corporations varied to the extent authority was centralized or decentralized, but all operated on the premise that the sheer multitude and complexity of business activities demanded specialization of functions. Typically, then, finance, purchasing, sales, legal, engineering, and personnel departments evolved, with their own procedures, rules, regulations, and patterns of authority. Management—plant managers, superintendents, supervisors—increasingly became important, as a detailed division of labor grew on the factory floor and in the company office.

Consequently, labor requirements changed; the demand for professionals grew as did the demand for white-collar administrative and clerical staff. Attorneys with expertise in business law, university-trained engineers and scientists, as well as certified accountants found careers in corporations. As companies such as U.S. Steel, Ford, General Electric, and Standard Oil introduced welfare programs to promote loyalty among their employees, social workers, psychologists, and physicians joined the ranks of salaried personnel. The number of clerical workers needed to handle a variety of business transactions grew exponentially, and in the process clerical work became identified as "women's work." In 1870, there were approximately 11,000 female clerks, typists, and sales workers, representing less than one percent of all women employed in non-agricultural labor. By 1920, there were almost two million women employed in clerical and sales work, representing 26 percent of the nonagricultural female labor force.

The growth of nonproductive labor in corporations signified the formation of a middle class, based not on ownership of property (store, shop, or farm) but on knowledge, skill, education, and training. With the emergence of a "new" middle class, social stratification assumed different dimensions. White-collar and administrative workers, unlike even the most skilled manual worker among them, enjoyed steady employment, secure incomes, relatively short workdays, more favorable working conditions, and possessed clearly defined opportunities for promotion.

Such differences in the conditions and terms of employment translated into a disparity in living conditions. Cities became more sharply segregated by class, if not ethnicity and race. Industrial workers remained concentrated in the city center or the nearby surrounding area, while middle-class families resided miles from the city center; indeed, the relationship between income and place of residence became more direct as access to cheaper land and improvements in mass transit encouraged the development of suburbs. Surrounding Buffalo, Chicago, Cleveland, Pittsburgh, Toronto, and other industrial cities were "bedroom" communities whose residents worked in downtown offices, shopped in the centrally located department stores, and frequented the theaters, concert halls, and restaurants among the more fashionable parts of the city center. Social boundaries were accentuated by ostentatious displays of wealth in the city. Chicago's 200 millionaires, led by Marshall Field, owner of the nation's largest department store, resided on the "Gold Coast" along Lake Michigan; some, like Field's partner, Peter Palmer, were not satisfied with naming their homes, houses, or mansions, but instead opted for names like Palmer Palace.

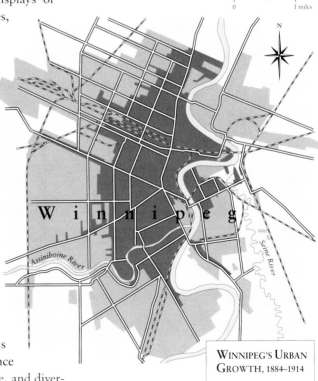

WINNIPEG'S URBAN GROWTH, 1884–1914

- urban area, 1884
- urban area, 1914
- main railroad by 1914

Similar developments occurred across North America among the newer cities, like Winnipeg in the prairie states and provinces and cities along the Pacific West Coast. In this respect, one could underscore the nationalization of life, as reflected in the shared experience of industrialization and urbanization. The "West," customarily viewed as a region that epitomized rural, agrarian society, should more appropriately be understood as a stage of development in which subsistence farming gave way to commercial agriculture, and diversified manufacturing accompanied the extraction of minerals and other natural resources. Railroads crisscrossed the Great Plains and the Rocky Mountains carrying people, goods, and information over great distances, and in the process made regional and national boundaries less meaningful.

The development of mass production methods and the growth of mass markets reinforced the social and economic integration that characterized an industrializing and urbanizing society. Corporations assumed strategic control of the core industries, initially steel, oil, and mining, and then automobile and electrical goods manufacturing. They effectively operated in national markets, and by World War I, their scope of activities assumed transnational proportions.

Corporations apparently personified the expansion of an industrial capitalist economy—greater levels of productivity resulting in an abundance of affordable consumer goods and accordingly a higher standard of living for those gainfully employed. Corporations were models of administrative efficiency, to be emulated by government institutions, civic bodies, and voluntary organizations. Their leaders spoke with authority and exerted considerable influence over public policy if not the political process itself. In short, the power of corporations was unmistakable—penetrating virtually every sphere of society—and therefore taken seriously by their boosters and critics alike.

As North Americans encountered an industrializing and urbanizing society, they did so with a mixture of anticipation and trepidation. On one hand, the hustling and bustling activity of rapidly growing cities like Chicago, described by the poet Carl Sandburg as "hog butcher for the world; toolmaker, stacker of wheat," embodied the country's economic prowess, which in turn purportedly reflected traits of a national character—a drive to succeed and an ability to seize on each and every opportunity to do so. Andrew Carnegie went even further, attributing American cities' achievements in the arts, commerce, transportation, communication, and governance as indicative of a "triumphant democracy." In this context neither industrialization nor urbanization was problematic; indeed, both seemed to fulfill the promise of American society.

Maxwell Street, Chicago, almost a replica of a European market place, familiar to the many immigrants in this busy scene.

New methods of construction allowed buildings to go higher.. This new office block, built of steel and concrete, on the corner of O'Farrall and Market Streets in San Francisco, was completed in 1925.

Other voices could be heard, however, raising questions about the consequences of these twin megadevelopments. In *Progress and Poverty* (1879), Henry George expressed alarm about monopolies and the diminishing opportunities for social and economic independence. Henry Demerest Lloyd, in *Wealth and Commonwealth* (1894), challenged the view that what was beneficial for corporate America was beneficial for the country at large. Lincoln Steffens, in a series of biting articles entitled "Shame of the Cities" (1904), published by *McClure's*, a magazine with a circulation of 750,000, took issue with the abuse of the public's trust by municipal officials who used their offices as vehicles for personal gain. Collectively, these critics called on their readers to reexamine their assumptions about the natural order of things, and to reject the complacency of those with perhaps the most to gain from portraying industrial capitalism and urbanization as unqualifiable blessings.

Looking backward, it is helpful to consider the forces transforming American society between 1870 and 1920 as neither impersonal nor inexorable. Innovation in transportation, communication, production, and organization involved purposeful human activity. City dwellers faced the demands of urban life by seeking to make densely populated areas into comfortable cosmopolitan communities. Citizens, quasicitizens (disenfranchised southern blacks and women), and noncitizens (unnaturalized immigrants) alike, aroused by their firsthand experience as workers, consumers, and ethnic and racial minorities, asserted their rights, and demanded rights formerly denied them, to claim their positions in an industrializing and urbanizing society.

LIFE ON THE GREAT PLAINS

The late nineteenth century witnessed the final destruction of traditional Native American cultures. White expansion headed across the continent, bringing conflict with tribes on the Great Plains of the trans-Mississippi West. This vast environment had been known as the Great American Desert, and was thought inhospitable for settlement, but the discovery of gold and silver and the construction of railroads turned attention toward the last remaining Indian stronghold.

Plains Indians were well aware of white society, which had been developing to the east. The extra mobility provided by horses, which probably came from Spanish sources sometime in the early 1700s, had greatly enhanced the traditional way of life.

Conflict began on pioneer trails heading to California. The Gold Rush of 1849 prompted thousands to travel overland, through the heart of Indian territory. Periodic rushes followed as rumors of gold deposits brought normally cautious prospectors deep into unchartered areas. Two government bills also stimulated western movement. In the United States the Homestead Act of 1862 gave 160 acres of land to any individual in return for $10 and a promise to cultivate the land for at least five years. In the same year, the Pacific Railroad Act authorized the construction of rail tracks connecting the Atlantic and Pacific coasts, granting some 170 million acres of land for development.

Conflict tended to flare up periodically as the strongest tribes repelled intruders, who were often entering territory granted in treaties with government officials. As the violence escalated, initial restraint and negotiation were replaced by a remorseless struggle that saw the massacre of women and children and the destruction of Indian camps and supplies. In 1864, at Sand Creek, Colorado, 450 Indians were killed after peacefully assembling for conciliatory talks by an army unit flying the white flag. The Indians' most famous victory came at the Battle of Little Big Horn, June 25, 1876; 225 members of the Seventh Cavalry, under George Armstrong Custer's leadership, were killed in a foolish attack on a huge Sioux encampment.

The government's Bureau of Indian Affairs tried to find a solution to the problem. A number of treaties were signed, but the problem was one of enforcement, as both whites and Indians paid little attention to agreements made. The 1867 *Report on the Condition of the Indian Tribes* recommended a new strategy of relocation to reservations, by force if necessary, as negotiation was not working. Tribes that had not already agreed to move to reservations were now coerced into doing so. Attitudes toward Indians as savages had inevitably hardened during the bitter fighting of the Plains Wars. In addition, a deliberate policy of slaughtering buffalo struck at the heart of the native economy, as once-massive herds were almost wiped out. Plains Indians were left with little choice but to accept relocation. In Canada, assimilation was the preferred method of dealing with Native peoples. The 1857 Act spelled out the process: "Act for the Gradual Civilization of the Indian Tribes in the Canadas."

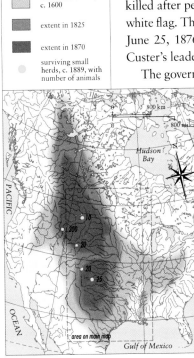

RANGE OF THE BUFFALO

maximum extent, c. 1600

extent in 1825

extent in 1870

surviving small herds, c. 1889, with number of animals

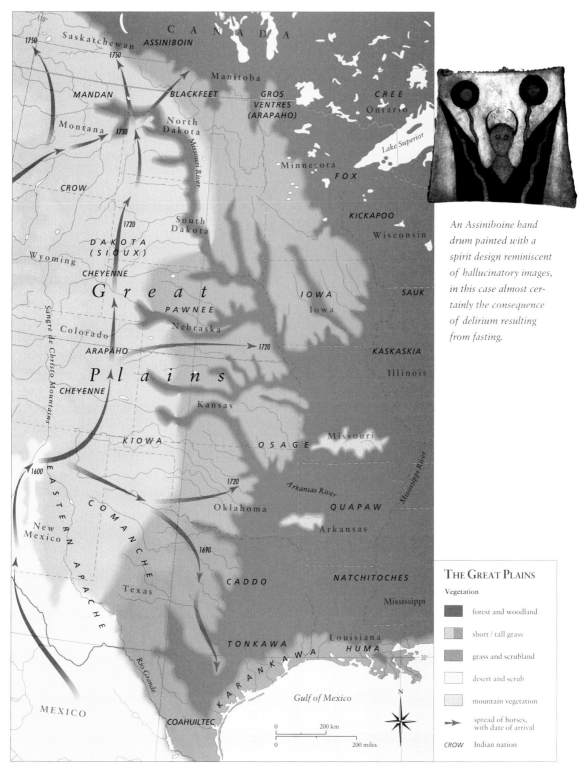

1750

Saskatchewan   ASSINIBOIN

1750

MANDAN   BLACKFEET   GROS   CREE
                        VENTRES   Ontario
Montana   North   (ARAPAHO)
          Dakota   Lake Superior
          1730
CROW   Minnesota   FOX

          South
          Dakota   KICKAPOO
          1720
WYOMING   DAKOTA   Wisconsin
          (SIOUX)

CHEYENNE

G r e a t   IOWA   SAUK
          PAWNEE   Iowa
Colorado Nebraska
ARAPAHO   1720   KASKASKIA

P l a i n s   Illinois
CHEYENNE
          Kansas

KIOWA   Missouri
          OSAGE

1600   1720   Arkansas River   Mississippi River
          Oklahoma   QUAPAW
New   Arkansas
Mexico   1690

          CADDO   NATCHITOCHES

          Texas

TONKAWA   Louisiana
          KARANKAWA HUMA
                              30

Rio Grande   Gulf of Mexico   N

MEXICO

COAHUILTEC   0   200 km
              0   200 miles

An Assiniboine hand
drum painted with a
spirit design reminiscent
of hallucinatory images,
in this case almost cer-
tainly the consequence
of delirium resulting
from fasting.

THE GREAT PLAINS

Vegetation

▮ forest and woodland

▮ short / tall grass

▮ grass and scrubland

▢ desert and scrub

▯ mountain vegetation

→ spread of horses,
   with date of arrival

CROW Indian nation

THE GOLDEN SPIKE

In May 1869, at Promontory Point, Utah, representatives from the Central Pacific and Union Pacific railroad companies took turns in driving the "golden spike" and thereby commemorated the completion of the first transcontinental railroad. Seven years after Congress authorized the project and subsidized the companies to the tune of $20 million and sixty million acres of land, the foundations of a national railway system were established. In subsequent decades, construction would accelerate as investments from financial capitalists in the eastern United States and their counterparts in Great Britain and France made the railways the largest of enterprises in an industrializing economy and their owners the wealthiest and most powerful men in the nation. Whereas on the eve of the Civil War, 30,000 miles of track had been laid, by the end of the century over 190,000 miles of track had been put down, and five transcontinental railroads were in operation.

For many contemporaries of the late nineteenth century and historians since then, the growth of railroads epitomized the comprehensive transformation of the United States from a rural, agricultural society to an urban, industrial society. Railroads linked the growers of wheat and the raisers of livestock with flour mills in Minneapolis and meatpacking plants in Kansas City. Railroads not only facilitated production by transporting unfinished goods to manufacturing centers; they also promoted the development of mass markets for consumer goods. Potato farmers in Idaho could furnish their households through purchases from mail-order catalogues from Montgomery Ward and Sears Roebuck in Chicago. The development of markets in turn implied the movement of people. Railroads fueled the rapid settlement of the trans-Mississippi West after the Civil War, as migrants from points farther east, including immigrants from Europe, were lured by prospects of

"In the ripeness of time the hope of humanity is realized . . . this continental railway . . . will bind the two seaboards to this one continental union like ears to the human head; to plant the foundation of the Union so broad and deep . . . that no possible force or stratagem can shake its permanence."
William Gilpin, author of *The Cosmopolitan Railway,* 1890

obtaining land, establishing a lucrative business, and securing steady and remunerative employment. Between 1870 and 1900, over two million immigrants alone were able to resettle within the area covering the Great Plains and what soon became known as the prairie states.

Above all, the railroad symbolized technical prowess, the genius of applied science and economic innovation celebrated by enthusiasts of material progress. From the introduction of improved techniques in the making of steel, to the construction of locomotive engines and the development of refrigerated cars, to transport cattle and farm produce, the railroad came to represent the cutting edge of industrialization.

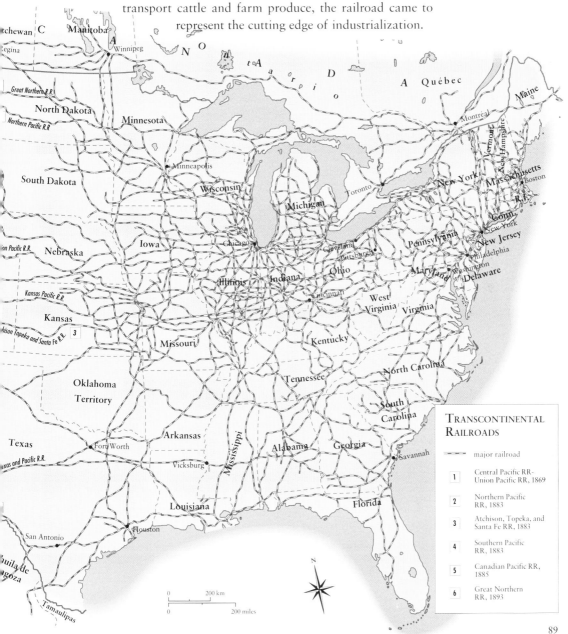

TRANSCONTINENTAL RAILROADS

- - -		major railroad
1		Central Pacific RR–Union Pacific RR, 1869
2		Northern Pacific RR, 1883
3		Atchison, Topeka, and Santa Fe RR, 1883
4		Southern Pacific RR, 1883
5		Canadian Pacific RR, 1885
6		Great Northern RR, 1893

THE WEST, 1865–1890

Wovoka, c. 1920

"When the sun died I went up to heaven and saw God and all the people who had died a long time ago. God told me to come back and tell my people they must be good and love one another, and not fight, or steal, or lie. He gave me this dance to give my people."
Wovoka, the Paiute prophet

After 1865, the shared belief that the country's future lay with settlement of the western lands beyond the Mississippi River became a living reality. Between 1865 and 1890, eight territories, like North and South Dakota, Montana, and Idaho, entered the Union as states not long after being opened for settlement.

For many North Americans and European observers, the West consisted of "virgin" lands—inhabited but undeveloped by indigenous peoples, a cornucopia of untapped natural resources and a vast frontier presenting challenges and opportunities for the restless, industrious, and motivated. Despite this idealized image, the energy applied by hundreds of thousands of settlers in mining, farming, and construction promoted the growth of commodity production and accelerated the industrialization of the national economy.

Between 1870 and 1890, the number of acres settled and cultivated in the United States, largely west of the Mississippi, exceeded the entire acreage opened to settlement over the previous 250 years. The number of farms tripled between 1870 and 1910, although in relative terms the proportion of the population who earned their livelihood from agriculture declined.

Along with this economic expansion came conflict over land use and ownership. Access to land by grazers and homesteaders was mainly limited to the rights of ownership, while during the 1870s and early 1880s, open-range cattle ranchers as well as sheepherders could effectively control as much as ten times the land they legally owned. Access to water also became a contentious issue; efforts to tap and rechannel water supply through irrigation and reclamation projects raised questions about ownership, and triggered the intervention of state and federal government to define water as a public resource.

Not surprisingly, the boundaries between private and public domain repeatedly shifted. Federal bureaus leased land in exchange for royalties, sold land at fixed prices, or otherwise granted lands to promote irrigation. Notwithstanding the provisions of laws authorizing such measures, most of this land fell into the hands of timber companies in the Pacific Northwest like Weyerhaeuser, southwestern copper magnates such as Anaconda and Phelps Dodge, and the Colorado gold and silver operations of the Consolidated Mining Company.

By 1893, the frontier was officially closed. Economic activity increasingly came under the direction of corporations. Towns like Butte, Montana, a copper mining center, were integrated from their very inception into a national chain of production and distribution. Some, like Denver, grew at a breathtaking pace. Founded during the Gold Rush of 1858–1860, by 1880 Denver had become the largest city between Kansas City and San Francisco, and ten years later, its population had tripled to 107,000.

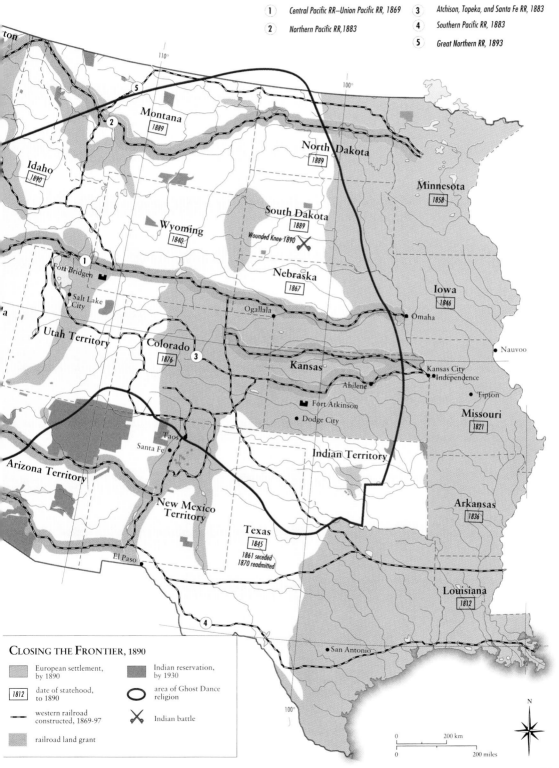

① Central Pacific RR–Union Pacific RR, 1869   ③ Atchison, Topeka, and Santa Fe RR, 1883

② Northern Pacific RR, 1883   ④ Southern Pacific RR, 1883

⑤ Great Northern RR, 1893

Montana
1889

Idaho
1890

North Dakota
1889

Minnesota
1858

Wyoming
1840

South Dakota
1889

Wounded Knee 1890 ✕

Fort Bridger

Salt Lake City

Utah Territory

Nebraska
1867

Ogallala

Omaha

Iowa
1846

Nauvoo

Colorado
1876

Kansas

Kansas City
Independence

Abilene

Tipton

Fort Atkinson

Dodge City

Missouri
1821

Taos
Santa Fe

Indian Territory

Arizona Territory

New Mexico
Territory

Arkansas
1836

Texas
1845
1861 seceded
1870 readmitted

El Paso

Louisiana
1812

San Antonio

CLOSING THE FRONTIER, 1890

European settlement, by 1890

Indian reservation, by 1930

1812 date of statehood, to 1890

area of Ghost Dance religion

western railroad constructed, 1869-97

✕ Indian battle

railroad land grant

N

0   200 km

0   200 miles

THE RISE OF BUSINESS

Industrialization is associated with technological innovation—the introduction of more efficient methods of production, transportation, and communication, along with mechanization. Yet central to industrialization was another form of innovation—organizational in character—that saw the evolution of institutional structures and practices that emanated from, and reinforced, the development of mass markets and mass production. This was reflected when in 1896 the mass of industrial workers voted for a pro-business presidential candidate, William McKinley.

Between 1870 and 1920, larger-scale enterprises, measured in terms of the number of employees, output, and capital, assumed a strategic position within the nation's economy. The scale of operations facilitated efficiencies in production and distribution that resulted in lower per unit costs and earned larger enterprises greater shares of the market.

Andrew Carnegie, the owner, and Henry Clay Frick, the director of the Carnegie Iron and Steel Company's largest plant in Homestead, Pennsylvania, systematically and single-mindedly deployed the Bessemer process in the making of steel, which enabled the firm to substitute less skilled and lower-paid operatives for highly skilled molders and puddlers. Moreover, the company gained control of the supply of iron ore and coal, and thereby was able to undersell its competitors. In 1901, with the backing of J. P. Morgan, a New York finance capitalist, Carnegie's company became U.S. Steel, the world's largest industrial enterprise, which claimed almost two-thirds of the national steel market.

In other industries a form of horizontal integration proceeded relentlessly as firms eliminated competition through mergers and acquisitions. By the turn of the century, such corporations as the American Tobacco Company, the American Sugar Company, and the American Can Company dominated their respective industrial markets. The most conspicuous example of this process was Standard Oil, under the direction of John D. Rockefeller, which in 1882 claimed 90 percent of all the oil extracted and refined in the United States, and accordingly became the target of those alarmed by the influence of "trusts" and "monopolies" in the American economy.

In a fundamental sense, the forerunners of the modern corporation were the railway companies, which by virtue of the scale and scope of their operations developed an organizational structure that enabled greater coordination and control over a complex array of activities. Since the companies provided passenger, freight, and postal service spanning thousands of miles, more attention had been devoted to the management of

THE VOTE FOR BUSINESS

Presidential vote by county, 1896

- states decisive to the outcome of the election
- McKinley, Republican
- Bryan, Democrat
- territory not voting

specialized activities, such as preparing timetables, billing customers, monitoring ticket sales, maintaining rolling stock, yards, and stations, and recruiting, training, and overseeing labor. A breakdown in any of these functions could threaten the profit-making ability of the business.

Big business was "big" not only because of its capital reserves, volume of sales, or profit rate; the organizational resources at its disposal allowed big business to exercise disproportionate power at the workplace, in the market, and, for some observers, in society at large. For Americans traditionally wary of the concentration of power in any form, this represented an alarming development.

A huge steel plant mass producing rail tracks, using the latest industrial methods.

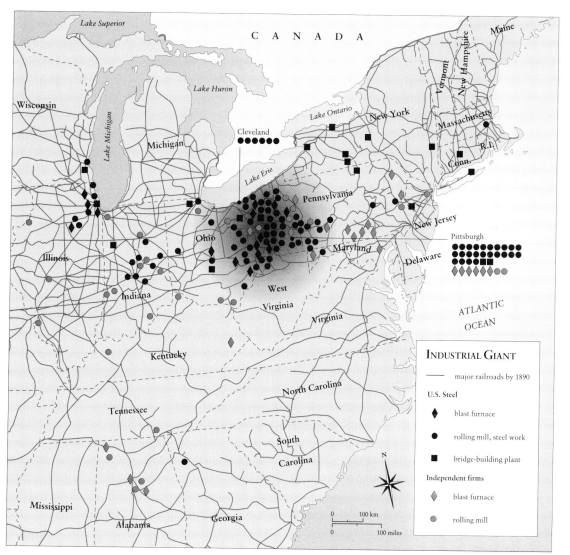

INDUSTRIAL GIANT

— major railroads by 1890

U.S. Steel

◆ blast furnace

● rolling mill, steel work

■ bridge-building plant

Independent firms

◆ blast furnace

● rolling mill

THE RISE OF LABOR

The earliest trade unions, commonly journeymen societies, could be traced to the antebellum period in commercial centers such as New York, Philadelphia, and Boston. Almost without exception they formed locally based organizations and were short-lived.

In the 1860s, a new generation of unions emerged, led by British, Irish, and German immigrants or their native-born offspring. Their membership was almost exclusively drawn from the ranks of skilled workers: machinists, molders, printers (compositors and pressmen), building tradesmen, and cigar makers. These unions were organized by craft, along the lines of specialized lines of work, so that although bricklayers, carpenters, and plumbers, for example, worked on the same construction site, they belonged to different unions.

By the 1890s, however, some workers had begun to organize by industry. For instance, members of the individual craft-based unions on the railroads, such as the Brotherhood of Locomotive Firemen, the Brotherhood of Locomotive Engineers, and the Brotherhood of Conductors, combined to form the American Railway Union (ARU) on the strategic premise that only a national industrial union could muster the strength to deal with the railroad companies. The ARU passed its first test when, in 1894, striking members forced James Hill, owner of the Great Northern Railway, to rescind the third in a series of wage cuts. However, later that year, the ARU felt the wrath of the U.S. government when the union organized a labor boycott against any railway using Pullman passenger cars, in support of Pullman employees striking against the company's decision to cut wages. Court-imposed injunctions, combined with stiff fines and the imprisonment of ARU leaders, crushed the strike/boycott and critically wounded the union.

During this period, trade unionists made special efforts to form national labor organizations to support the activities of individual craft and industrial unions. Between 1865 and 1872, under the leadership of Ira Steward, a machinist, and William Sylvis, a molder, the National Labor Union (NLU) encouraged the creation of producer cooperatives and pressed for prohibition of the use of contract labor and the establishment of an eight-hour work day.

After the NLU's demise, most unions either fended for themselves or maintained a loose connection to the Knights of Labor (KOL). From its inception in 1869 until the mid-1880s, the KOL experienced little growth. Then membership skyrocketed, as a result of a successful strike mobilized by KOL assemblies, consisting of railway workers employed on the Wabash line owned by Jay Gould; later, however, the KOL suffered a damaging setback at the hands of Gould's Missouri Pacific line when striking laborers, many of them African American, were permanently sacked. KOL membership spread to Canada after 1881.

In 1886, leaders of craft unions, such as Samuel Gompers (Cigar Makers International Union) and Peter McGuire (United Brotherhood of Carpenters and Joiners), dissatisfied with the Knights of Labor, helped to establish the American Federation of Labor (AFL), which soon became the largest national labor organization. Affiliates of the AFL, unlike the KOL, tended to exclude less skilled factory operatives, especially women and recently arrived immigrants from Southern and Eastern Europe. Some, through high dues rates and initiation fees or bylaws, effectively excluded African Americans from membership. The United Mine Workers was one of the few unions to deviate from this norm, as its organizing campaigns in the anthracite coal fields in the late 1890s included Slavic immigrants, and its efforts among bituminous-coal miners intermittently led to the emergence of biracial unions in West Virginia and Alabama.

The AFL's leadership of the labor movement, however, did not go uncontested. Veterans of labor struggles in the 1890s, many from the lumber and mining camps in the west, formed the Industrial Workers of the World (IWW). Organizers envisioned the creation of "One Big Union" uniting workers irrespective of race, ethnicity, and gender, and advanced a strategy of direct action at the workplace not only to press employers for higher wages and better conditions but to establish workers' control of industry itself. The IWW was active among woolen textile workers in Massachusetts, silk workers in New Jersey, dock workers in Philadelphia, timber workers in Louisiana and Oklahoma, agricultural workers in Kansas, Nebraska, and California, copper miners in Arizona and Montana, and lumber workers in Washington. Subject to state repression during World War I and the subsequent "Red Scare" of 1919–1921, the IWW precipitously declined in influence. Not until the 1930s, with the rise of a new labor federation, the Congress of Industrial Organizations, would many of these workers return to the membership of unions.

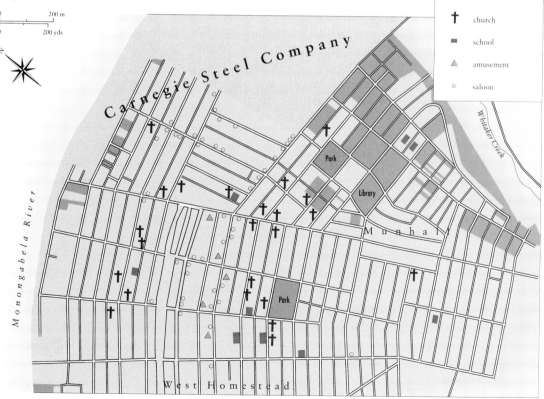

HOMESTEAD: A
WORKER'S TOWN

Carnegie Steel Co.

Carnegie Steel Co. housing

railroad

road

✝ church

■ school

▲ amusement

○ saloon

IMMIGRATION, 1850–1920

DESTINATION OF CANADIAN EMIGRANTS TO THE UNITED STATES, 1890–1914

Total: 435,000

rest of United States

western states

Boston and New England

Midwest

Detroit

rest of the New York state

New York City

By the mid-nineteenth century, immigration had been recognized as part and parcel of the continent's growth, even if the host population was ambivalent about the newcomers' effects on American institutions and culture. Developments in Europe spurred well over a million Germans, Irish, and British to migrate to the United States by 1850, whether they were the fallout of the 1848 revolutions, the crisis in artisanal craft production, the Irish potato famine, or the glutted labor markets of English and Scottish towns and villages. That the numbers of German, Irish, and British migrants entering the United States continued unabated until 1890 suggested that longer-term social, economic, and political changes in Northern and Western Europe, combined with the demands of the industrializing American economy, made migration a viable option. Only the Civil War and the protracted depressions of 1873–1887 and 1893–1897 slowed down the rates of immigration.

Persistent too was the proclivity of certain immigrant groups to settle in specific areas of the United States. The Irish, despite their rural peasant backgrounds, gravitated to manufacturing cities and seaports, such as New York, Philadelphia, Boston, Chicago, and San Francisco, and mining towns like Butte, Montana, and Denver, Colorado. German communities flourished in such industrial centers as Chicago, St. Louis, and Cincinnati as well as Midwestern farmlands.

These tendencies continued even as the pattern of immigration began to change after 1890. From then on, the majority of immigrants originated from Italy, czarist Russia (including the Baltic States, Poland, and Finland), and Austria-Hungary, a multinational empire consisting of Czechs, Slovaks, and Croatians, to name a few. Wracked by social upheaval and political turmoil emanating from the shift from subsistence to commercial agriculture, uneven industrialization, and the pressures posed by accelerating rates of population

As the major focus of immigration to North America shifted from northwestern to southeastern Europe, not all approved, as demonstrated by this cartoon dating from 1891, The Evils of Unrestricted Immigration.

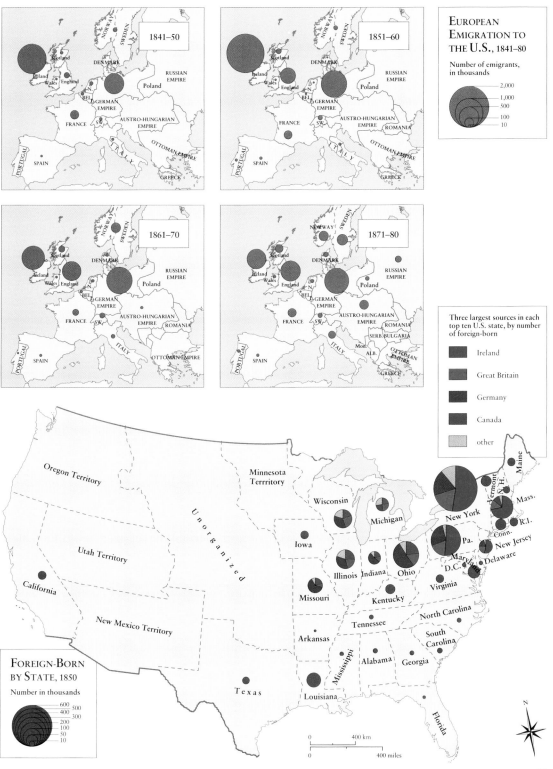

EUROPEAN EMIGRATION TO THE U.S., 1841–80

Number of emigrants, in thousands

2,000
1,000
500
100
10

1841–50

1851–60

1861–70

1871–80

Three largest sources in each top ten U.S. state, by number of foreign-born

Ireland

Great Britain

Germany

Canada

other

FOREIGN-BORN BY STATE, 1850

Number in thousands

600
500
400
300
200
100
50
10

0   400 km

0   400 miles

A first taste of America. This group of immigrants was photographed taking a meal at Ellis Island, New York, August 1923.

growth, Europe experienced a wave of migrations—internal (from the country-side to the town and from eastern and southern areas to northern and western regions of the continent) and external (emigration to the Western Hemisphere).

Between 1890 and 1920, more than eighteen million Europeans emigrated to the United States, the largest single recipient of an increasingly mobile population, driven by economic necessity, political repression, and religious persecution. These "new" immigrants, just as their Western and Northern European predecessors did, concentrated in the nation's expanding cities. In New York, Little Italy coexisted with Kleindeutschland (Little Germany), and Manhattan's Lower East Side became the home of more Jews than any other city in the world. In Chicago, Polish, Czech, and Scandinavian enclaves emerged, each indicating in their own distinct ways the importance of "Old World" cultures even as the newcomers acculturated to life in their adopted homelands.

In 1920, when the U.S. Census showed that for the first time the majority of the country's population lived in cities and American industrial power continued its ascendancy within the international economy, immigrants' place in urban and industrial America became more transparent. As politicians and social commentators debated the society's ability to integrate the new immigrants, their contribution to every sphere of life was unmistakable. Manufacturing and extractive industries heavily depended on the skills and sheer muscle of immigrants and their native-born sons and daughters. Their input energized mass entertainment, created for a consuming public that possessed more leisure time—be it motion pictures, popular music, comedy, or sports. Even as Congress passed the National Origins Act (1924) to curb immigration in response to pressure from nativist groups, the fact remained that the United States was a nation of immigrants and their American-born offspring.

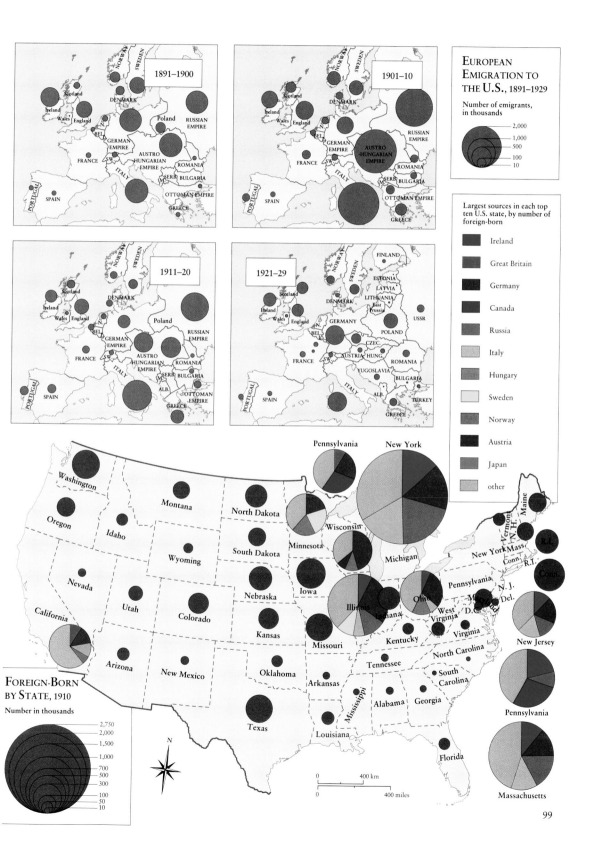

EUROPEAN EMIGRATION TO THE U.S., 1891–1929

Number of emigrants, in thousands

2,000
1,000
500
100
10

Largest sources in each top ten U.S. state, by number of foreign-born

Ireland
Great Britain
Germany
Canada
Russia
Italy
Hungary
Sweden
Norway
Austria
Japan
other

1891–1900

1901–10

1911–20

1921–29

FOREIGN-BORN BY STATE, 1910

Number in thousands

2,750
2,000
1,500
1,000
700
500
300
100
50
10

0   400 km

0   400 miles

Pennsylvania

New Jersey

Massachusetts

URBAN LIFE, 1900–1930

Cities grew throughout the nineteenth century, but between 1870 and 1920 in particular their rate of growth accelerated, and they developed features that distinguished them from their older preindustrial predecessors. Whereas in 1870, six North American cities claimed a population of at least 250,000, by 1920, twenty-five cities held that distinction. In 1880, only in the state of Massachussetts did 60 percent of the population live in urban communities, but by 1920, this was true for residents of ten other states. New cities rose to challenge the preeminent position of the eastern seaports of New York, Philadelphia, and Boston, and such river cities as New Orleans, Montréal, St. Louis, and Cincinnati. The population of Los Angeles, California, jumped from 11,200 in 1870 to 319,000 in 1920, on the eve of the "Automobile Age." Seattle, Washington, constituted only a town in 1880 with a population of 3,500, but by 1910, it was the third largest city on the Pacific Coast, with 237,000 inhabitants.

Such considerable growth stemmed in large measure from improvements in transportation. Railroads quickly supplanted horsecars and omnibuses, and were accompanied by cable cars, electric streetcars, and, in New York, by an elaborate underground rail system. Innovation in transportation especially helped foster the growth of suburbs, satellite communities around the city. In Boston, for example, almost three-quarters of its population lived within a three-mile radius of the city's center in 1850, but with the expansion of the railway and streetcar network, that number had dropped to only 60 percent by 1900. Propelling this process was the appearance of the automobile as an affordable means of transport after 1920. Vigorously deploying the methods of assembly line production, the Ford Motor Company helped make the Model T the symbol of the nation's prosperous and mobile population. In due order came a feverish speculation in Florida and

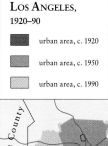

LOS ANGELES, 1920–90

- urban area, c. 1920
- urban area, c. 1950
- urban area, c. 1990

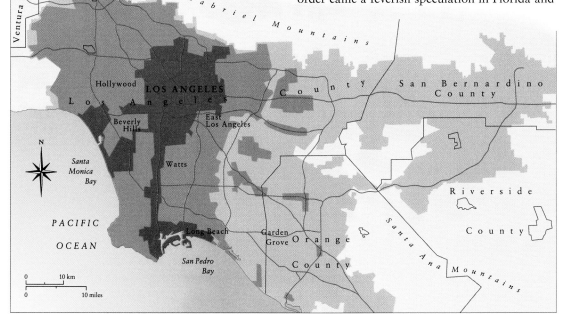

California real estate in anticipation of new residents, the opening of the first suburban shopping center (the precursor of the modern mall), and the development of the first fast-food chain, A & W Root Beer in Kansas City.

Despite the dispersal of residential communities, the urban population remained relatively concentrated. Since land was at a premium, many cities accommodated growing populations by building upward. Multiple dwelling units called tenement houses, typically the homes of recently arrived immigrants and lower-paid manual workers, emerged in New York, Chicago, and Boston, to the consternation of the middle-class observers who regarded this housing as a breeding ground of disease, crime, and poverty.

Public health concerns were not restricted to tenement house conditions. Inadequate attention to the disposal of sewage led to outbreaks of diphtheria and typhoid in Chicago between 1884 and 1891; only with the completion of the Ship and Sanitary Canal in 1899, which reversed the flow of the Chicago River, did city authorities gain control over the problem. In city after city, public initiatives accompanied private efforts to establish dispensaries, clinics, and hospitals in recognition that communicable diseases were more virulent in a densely populated environment.

Almost universal to urban life were the urgent calls to "civilize" the city. These entailed the need to "police the masses" whose "criminal" and "immoral" behavior combined with a demand to professionalize the police forces and rid them of corruption. Accordingly, the New York Society for the Suppression of Vice (1872) and the City Vigilance League (1894) waged campaigns against prostitution, gambling, and excessive drinking, and civic leaders after 1895 began to strip politicians' authority to make appointments to the police force and introduced more objective hiring procedures.

Others answered the call differently. In New York the Charity Organization Society dispensed advice to the poor about how to better manage their lives, and the Institutional Church League, practicing a form of "social gospel," built recreational facilities and conducted training programs to uplift the poor.

Such initiatives suggested that the urban environment was a wilderness that could be transformed. In newer and older cities alike, funds were raised and allocated for the construction of parks, commons, squares, boulevards, and fountains in the hope of "beautifying" the city. As Chicago and New York built upward with the advent of "skyscrapers," the importance of preserving if not creating public space for the common enjoyment of the urbanite gained sway.

In this way the urban population attempted to reconcile modern lifestyles with traditional values identified with rural patterns of living. This persistent ambivalence, expressed in the allure of urbanity along with the fear that society was losing its innocence, struck a chord in many North Americans, especially since the population of cities continued to swell with recently arrived immigrants and internal migrants who came mainly from rural backgrounds. Not surprisingly, the growth and development of an urban society produced tensions, which resonated in the political and social movements of the period.

With the completion of the Canadian Pacific Railroad and the Panama Canal, Vancouver increasingly became the conduit of goods and commmerce for western Canada, and grew rapidly between 1880 and 1920.

POPULISTS AND PROGRESSIVES

The rural ideal? In fact, the reality for many rural families faced with falling prices could be very different. In bad years, the cost of producing a crop might not be recovered from its sale on the market.

The Populist and Progressive movements arose from Americans' efforts to confront the challenges of industrialization and urbanization. Each in its own way sought to reform American institutions with the aim of reaffirming traditional values. Each stressed the need for an "activist" state to correct inequities, redress grievances, and curb the growth of concentrated and unaccountable power. Each sought to come to grips with the development of corporate capitalism and its implications for the position of farmers, small businessmen, and workers in a market economy.

Populism represented a crystallization of farmers' movements dating back to the 1870s, which through self-help, agitation, lobbying, and political action sought to exert control of the vagaries of the market. Farmers sold their produce in highly competitive markets but bought what was necessary to sustain a farm in less competitive markets; consequently, between 1884 and 1907, their income fell below their expenditures of consumer goods. The Populist movement garnered support from wheat growers in the Midwest, especially Iowa, Kansas, and Nebraska, and among

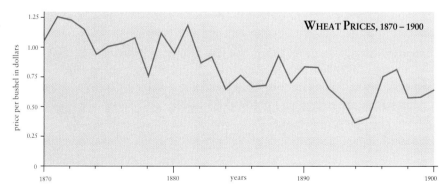

cotton growers in the South, who despite different agricultural systems shared concerns about ready access to credit and curbs on the practices of railway operators.

The Populists, building on the strength of the northern and southern Farmers' Alliances, organized the People's Party (Populist) in 1892 on a program calling for government ownership of the railroads and telephone industry, a government-funded credit system whereby farmers could borrow up to 80 percent of the market value of their crops, paper currency based on silver instead of gold, and a set of political reforms, including the direct election of U.S. senators and the adoption of the Australian (secret) ballot.

In 1892, candidates of the People's Party won gubernatorial elections in Kansas, Nebraska, and Colorado as well as capturing five seats in the Senate and ten in the House of Representatives. That same year, James Weaver, the party's candidate for president, won 8 percent of the popular vote, and twenty-two electoral votes.

Progressivism, unlike Populism, was not a unitary movement, but really a series of issue-orientated campaigns. Unlike the farmers' movement of the 1880s and 1890s, its base of support was in the country's cities, whose rate of growth continued unabated in the early twentieth century. Progressives did share with Populists a belief that state intervention, particularly at the level of the federal government, could effectively address society's ills. Accordingly, they successfully pressed for measures to protect the rights of consumers, conserve the natural environment, monitor the behavior of dominant corporations, or otherwise promote competition through the prohibition of unfair trade practices.

Progressives also assumed center stage in campaigns for "good, clean" municipal government in which the "civic-minded," disinterested professional would manage cities on principles similar to those of the efficient corporation. Many Progressives in midwestern and far western states mounted effective campaigns for democratic political reforms, including the adoption of referenda and initiatives that potentially provided the electorate a greater say over public policy.

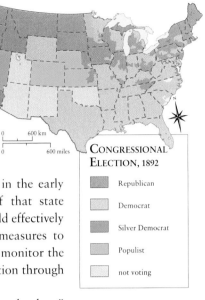

0   600 km
0   600 miles

CONGRESSIONAL ELECTION, 1892

Republican

Democrat

Silver Democrat

Populist

not voting

PRESIDENTIAL VOTE, 1892

Populist share of the vote, in percentage

48
30
15
5

not voting

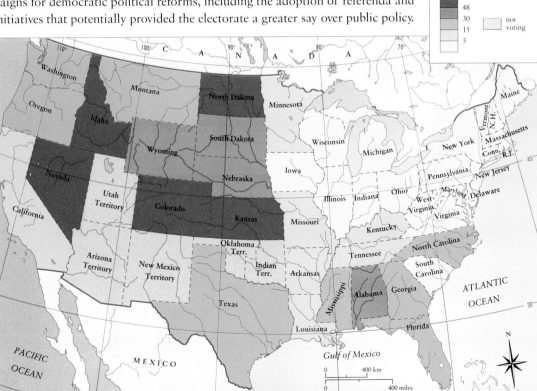

PART V: THE AMERICAN CENTURY

Just months prior to the U.S. entry into the Second World War, Henry Luce, publisher of *Life* magazine, proclaimed the twentieth century as the "American Century," not only because they happened to be a part of it, but also "because it is America's first century as a dominant power in the world." In the decades after the Civil War, the United States first consolidated its power and then grew rapidly in many respects. During the twentieth century, the U.S. initially embarked on an imperial surge, greatly increased its share of the world economy, and significantly shaped the conclusion of the First World War.

After the Wall Street crash of 1929, and most prominently during the 1930s, the United States pursued a limited form of isolationism. During and following the Second World War, the United States would realize its power, Luce thought, "for the purposes as we see fit and by such means as we see fit." The central concerns for Luce were that the United States should extend its economic model and its technical skills, provide aid, and ensure the success of liberty and justice around the globe. In many ways Luce assumed that the modernization of the world equated with its Westernization or Americanization. But even as the United States sought to extend its influence, or exert its power, or pursue globalization, there were always pockets of resistance to the trends of economic integration or to U.S. ideologies. Globalization was simultaneously accompanied by fragmentation.

The U.S. power base was laid in the post–Civil War period. Not only did the Union survive the attempted Southern secession, but it ultimately created a stronger nation. This vast land mass was both the source of extensive raw materials and ultimately a huge domestic market. The U.S. rapid industrial growth rivaled the growth of all of Europe in some products and sectors. The solid base of economic power was by the 1890s accompanied by a significant growth in the U.S. Navy, built at the behest of Alfred Thayer Mahan and Theodore Roosevelt. The U.S. rise to globalism was simultaneously accompanied by the relative decline of the "old" European colonial powers. Spain was visibly defeated in the 1898 wars in Cuba and the Philippines, and even the most significant European colonial power, Britain, was in relative decline.

Rightly or not, the rapid growth and hyperproductivity in the late nineteenth century impelled a more active foreign policy on the part of Washington in search of new markets for U.S. products. The Open Door declaration by the United States that it wanted all ports of China to be open for trade, and the more general open markets for U.S. economic activity constituted, in the words of historian Howard Zinn, "a more sophisticated approach to imperialism than traditional empire-building of Europe." U.S. exports increased sevenfold during the decades around the turn of the century, and ultimately U.S. diplomacy would vigorously try to protect the increased tendency toward further economic integration and later globalization. The third of President Wilson's Fourteen Points included the injunction to remove economic barriers around the world. The United States enjoyed huge economies of scale, given the size and relative wealth of their domestic economy and market. Carnegie Steel was producing more than Britain; U.S. per capita income was far higher than that of the other great powers. In many respects the U.S. power was rivaling that of the continent of Europe. Four hundred years of European dominance of the world economy ended with World War I, the "Great War."

Alternative interpretations exist on how to characterize the U.S. economic expansion of the period. Some historians regard the U.S. experience of imperialism or the operation of hegemony in the Western Hemisphere as benevolent in intention. Diplomacy sometimes acquired the adjectives "welfare" or "Samaritan," or was said to be "missionary" in nature, imperialism harnessing the progressive ideas of the period. Others contend that the United States used its economic muscle to gain political advantage, expanding its power into the corners of the globe. The idea of isolationism could not be sustained against the background of daily international trade.

Nevertheless, within the first half of the twentieth century, the United States pushed its interests to the fore, and within decades, U.S. production techniques and trade regulations became dominant.

The global political agenda was also heavily influenced by U.S. ideas and institutions. When the United States entered the First World War, Woodrow Wilson promised to make the "world safe for democracy" and promote "self-determination," at least for European nations. The Wilsonian agenda was eventually made explicit in his Fourteen Points speech of 1918, signaling a rival set of ideas to the writings and speeches of Lenin and Trotsky following the Russian Revolution. These ideas would ultimately become the basis of much political discourse in the latter part of the "American" century. Wilson intended to embody these formulations in the League of Nations (an international organization formed to solve problems by arbitration), which he proposed as the last of the Fourteen Points. Ultimately, however, the Senate rejected U.S. participation in the League. In many respects the post–World War II creation of the United Nations addressed the previous U.S. concerns, giving it a supreme position within the organization along with the other permanent members of the Security Council.

Still, there was considerable resistance to U.S. ambitions. Not all powers sought the extension of either democracy or self-determination. The European colonial powers held on to their "possessions" for as long as they could. Nationalist aspirations, some U.S. pressure, and the inability of the colonial powers to maintain their systems after World War II introduced an alternative characterization of the twentieth century. The century also became known as the "age of the masses." Furthermore, the U.S. ideals and ambitions were challenged by the rise of Nazism in Germany and the Nazi occupation of extensive sections of Europe, closing off these areas to the U.S. market. And in the Far East the extension of Japanese power from 1931 into China and then into Southeast Asia posed a significant obstacle to U.S. ambitions, which could ultimately be removed only through the U.S. entry into war in December 1941.

"The world must be made safe for democracy." *President Woodrow Wilson,* speech to Congress, 1917

SPANISH–AMERICAN WAR

Cuba had long been an object of U.S. consideration for inclusion in the Union. Despite relinquishing their holdings in the rest of Latin America, the Spanish held on to Cuba and the Philippines.

The cumulative effects of the U.S. recessions in the 1890s and the U.S. tariffs on Cuban produce (sugar) had an acute impact on the Cuban economy. By mid-decade, the revolts against the Spanish had gathered pace under José Martí. The revolts were subdued by the Spanish, who used concentration camps to control the Cuban nationals. Sentiment in the United States grew in support of assisting Cuba's liberation.

Cuban insurgents often destroyed U.S. property in an attempt to induce further U.S. participation against the Spanish, who were responsible for protecting the U.S. investments. The battleship USS Maine had moved into Havana harbor ostensibly to protect U.S. property and citizens. On February 15, 1898, the ship exploded, killing 260 crewmen on board. It was assumed at the time that the Spanish were responsible, and these assumptions were reinforced by sensational press reports. Later investigation put the explosion down to internal combustion. President William McKinley moved toward war with Spain. McKinley received a telegram from New York indicating: "Big corporations here now believe we will have war. Believe all would welcome it as a relief to suspense." Following the Spanish refusal to accept one of the U.S. conditions in negotiations, to grant independence to Cuba through U.S. mediation, McKinley obtained permission from Congress to take the United States to war on April 19, 1898. Senator Teller (from the sugar-producing state of Colorado) inserted an amendment that indicated that the United States did not seek to add Cuba to the Union.

Though the situation in Cuba instigated the Spanish-American War, the first action took place in the Philippines. Theodore Roosevelt, Assistant Secretary of the U.S. Navy, had earlier instructed Admiral Dewey to sail from Hong Kong to Manila should war with the Spanish break out. By the end of April 1898, Dewey had located the Spanish fleet south of Manila Bay because the Spanish commander had moved the ships to the shallowest point available to allow as many of his crew to survive, certain that the U.S. guns would prevail. Dewey sunk the fleet, killing 400. Though there was only one U.S. casualty in battle, over 2,000 would subsequently die from disease and rotten food. A further 400 U.S. casualties died in pursuit of the Filipino nationalist leader General Aguinaldo between 1898 and 1901, through the jungles and mountains of Luzon.

There remains disagreement on the U.S. motivations for capturing the Philippines. Was it just a by-product of the war with Spain, or did the islands provide the United States with a base from which to exert power in the region, especially in China to open up the "China Market?" Though the market was at

SPANISH FLEET DESTROYED IN MANILA BAY, 1898

- Spanish ship
- U.S. ship
- U.S. movement

that time relatively insignificant in comparison to the European, Latin American, and Canadian markets, the China market maintained an allure for U.S. politicians. The Philippines remained a U.S. colony until 1946.

The Spanish were also easily defeated in Cuba. Cuban nationalists controlled the interior of the island, forcing the Spanish to obtain their supplies by sea. The U.S. Navy patrolled and soon circled the island. Ultimately the Spanish fleet was blocked in Santiago Harbor by the end of May 1898. When the numerically superior U.S. forces arrived in Cuba in July, the infamous charge up Kettle and San Juan Hills, one led by Theodore Roosevelt's "Rough Riders," allowed the United States to dominate the garrison in Santiago. The Spanish fleet tried to escape from the harbor, but was soon destroyed. Ultimately Santiago surrendered on July 17, and the Spanish left Cuba in August.

Though the United States did not add territory to the Union at this point, it did become a colonial power for the next half century.

U.S. troops occupy trenches surrounding Manila, February 1899.

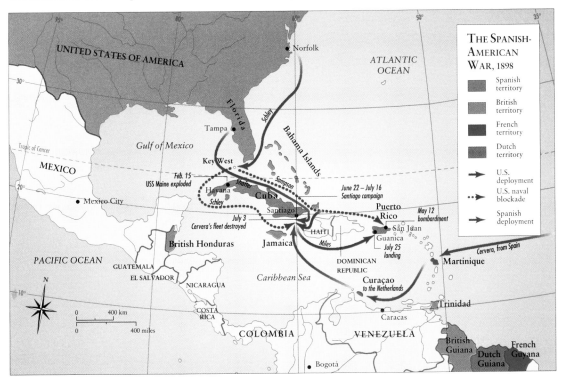

107

AGE OF EMPIRE

An illustration of the newly opened Panama Canal. Completed in 1914, its construction involved the removal of some 230 million cubic yards of earth and rock.

Through the later decades of the nineteenth century, the U.S. visions of empire moved more explicitly beyond their continental expansion. From the 1860s, U.S. Secretary of State William Seward had envisioned an empire from the Arctic in the north to Panama in the south, from Iceland in the east to Hawaii in the west. Such visions had been anticipated earlier by John Quincy Adams, and at times in the writings of Thomas Jefferson. By the end of the nineteenth century, the United States had the power to realize the vision.

Though the United States became a formal colonial power with the acquisition of the former Spanish-controlled areas, there was considerable resistance from the Anti-Imperial League to the further acquisition of territory. Anti-Imperialists contended, among many other reasons, that the peoples of the potential colonies had not given their consent to join the Union; that their inclusion would violate the Constitution; that imperialism was morally reprehensible; and that the Union should remain largely under white control.

Though formal imperialism was limited, a vigorous economic expansion was pursued through the policies derived from the Open Door notes issued by the McKinley administration. These notes insisted that the markets of China remain open to the United States, and that the territorial integrity of China be preserved from potential European colonization.

Historians vigorously disagree on the motivations for U.S. expansionism. On the one hand, they point to a benevolent mission to promote democracy, extend liberty, and protect U.S. security; on the other hand, revisionists point to the need to capture the markets and the resources of distant areas, without acquiring the reputation

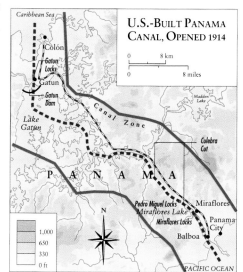

of being a colonial power.

Within the early decades of the twentieth century, U.S. power increased rapidly. Formal control was assumed in the Philippines and Puerto Rico, an informal hegemony was exercised over much of Central America, the Open Door policies were pursued in China, and though the market was perhaps illusionary, its appeal was still strong. President Theodore Roosevelt extended the meaning of the Monroe Doctrine, giving the United States the "right" to intervene in the internal affairs of the Latin American republics. Panama, a former province of Colombia, was wrested away with U.S. backing. The construction of the Panama Canal was completed in August 1914. The canal connected the Atlantic and Pacific Oceans, eliminating the need for shipping to take the long and dangerous route around South America. The great trading nations of Europe acquired a new route to the Pacific, and sea-borne trade between the East and West Coasts of the United States was made safer and more economical.

Within years, the United States would become a decisive influence in the outcome of the First World War, and move intermittently toward further globalization to assume a preponderant power in the Western orbit.

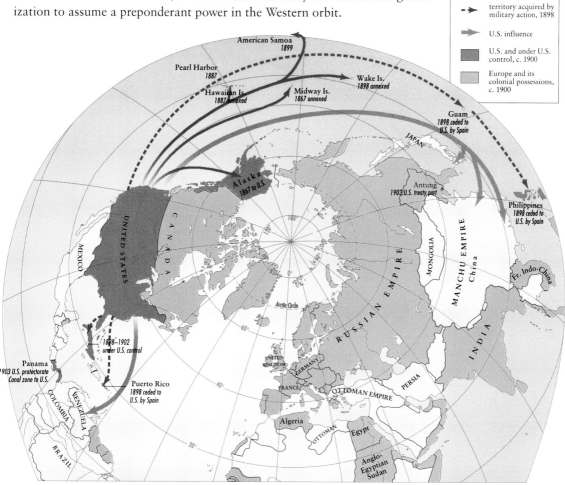

U.S. EXPANSION,
1867–1903

→ U.S. territorial expansion, 1867–99

⇢ territory acquired by military action, 1898

→ U.S. influence

▮ U.S. and under U.S. control, c. 1900

▮ Europe and its colonial possessions, c. 1900

American Samoa
1899

Pearl Harbor
1887

Wake Is.
1898 annexed

Hawaiian Is.
1887 annexed

Midway Is.
1867 annexed

Guam
1898 ceded to U.S. by Spain

JAPAN

Alaska
1867 to U.S.

Antung
1903 U.S. treaty port

Philippines
1898 ceded to U.S. by Spain

UNITED STATES

CANADA

MEXICO

MONGOLIA

MANCHU EMPIRE
China

Fr. Indo-China

RUSSIAN EMPIRE

INDIA

1898–1902 under U.S. control

UNITED KINGDOM

Panama
1903 U.S. protectorate Canal zone to U.S.

Puerto Rico
1898 ceded to U.S. by Spain

COLOMBIA

VENEZUELA

BRAZIL

FRANCE

GERMANY

PERSIA

OTTOMAN EMPIRE

Algeria

OTTOMAN

Egypt

Anglo-Egyptian Sudan

REVOLUTION IN MEXICO

The Mexican Revolution of 1910 was an event of seismic proportions for Mexico and Latin America, and it would have ramifications for U.S.-Mexican relations during the revolutionary period and after. The Revolution spawned a bloody civil war as well as internecine conflict among revolutionary factions, and the destruction in human life and property was staggering. Some estimates place the casualties at between one and two million combatants and civilians. If such figures are accurate, this was the bloodiest conflict in the history of the Americas.

The violent upheaval was a reflection of the acute political, economic, and social tensions of pre-revolutionary Mexico, which was under the thirty-five year rule of Porfirio Díaz and his technocratic advisers, who in the name of modernization and progress developed an economic program that benefitted only a small majority of Mexicans and foreigners. A broad spectrum of society—Indians, peasants, and workers—had their own grievances, while political liberals had taken exception to Díaz's U-turn on his promise to allow democratic elections for the presidency in 1910.

The uprising engineered by the the political liberal Francisco Madero in 1910 was the trigger for the conflict and the violence of the 1910s and the overspill of turbulence in the 1920s. Different revolutionary movements arose throughout the country and were temporarily united in their aim to overthrow the Díaz regime and its supporters. Once this was accomplished, the main revolutionary movements turned against each other. Two broad movements were of particular importance. In the south, Emilio Zapata led a peasant army with a mission to reclaim land appropriated from peasant and Indian communities during the Díaz era. Allied to Zapata was Pancho Villa and his private army in the northern region. Also in the north, Venustiano Carranza, a large landowner who supported Madero before his death at he hands of the counter-revolutionary general Victoriano Huerta, led an effective northern revolutionary army. By 1914 the forces of Carranza-led movement with its control of the railroads and the revenue of the Veracruz customs house gained the upper hand over Villa and over Zapata, who was later assassinated in 1919.

In a somewhat peripheral way, the United States was briefly drawn into the revolutionary tumult. President Wilson in 1914 ordered American marines to occupy the port of Veracruz with the avowed aim of toppling Huerta's counter-revolution. Also, in 1916, Wilson sent General Pershing and his forces into northern Mexico in a futile attempt to punish Pancho Villa for his raid on Columbus, New Mexico. Although Pershing's intervention had the tacit acceptance of Carranza, relations between Washington and the revolutionaries remained tense and unfriendly.

Essentially, the liberal agenda of the Mexican Revolution was able to dominate the more radical agrarian program. Even so, Carranza's forces at the constitutional assembly of 1916–1917 in Querétaro found it politic to agree to some of the far-reaching provisions of the Constitution of 1917, which set out revolutionary positions on such matters as land reform, workers' rights, national sovereignty over land and sub-soil rights, church–state relations among other things. The constitutional clause on the ownership of land and sub-soil deposits posed a threat to Americans and other foreigners who had acquired large units of land before the Revolution.

By the 1920s, most of the hard fighting was over but revolutionary turmoil continued. The political liberals who now dominated the Revolution had put the brakes on what could have been a much more radical social revolution. The order of the day was to consolidate the Revolution and to create more settled political and economic conditions. However, a revolutionary ideology now existed in the form of the Constitution of 1917 and during the 1930s, a time of depression and great want, there would be a renewed clamor for honoring the spirit of that great document, particularly in the matter of satisfying the hunger for land by peasant and Indian communities.

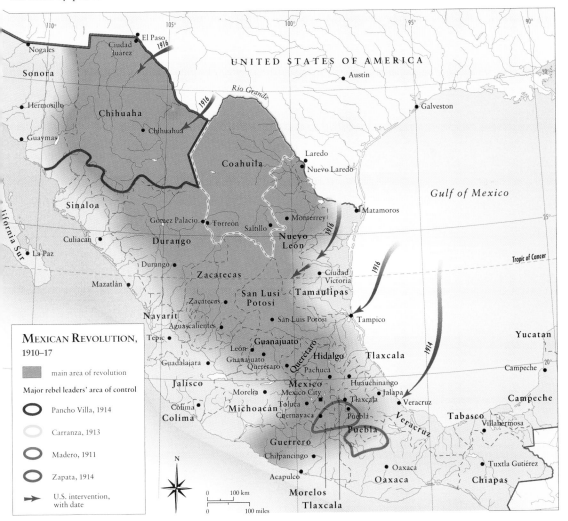

CANADA AND THE UNITED STATES IN WORLD WAR I

Canada had been directly involved in the First World War, as part of the British empire, from 1914. By 1917 the Allies had fought almost to exhaustion. In the fall of that year the first U.S. units arrived on the front line. The contribution made by the United States proved decisive. Here a 14-inch railroad gun opens fire in the Argonne, September 1918.

In 1914, Europe was locked together in a series of alliances, each intending to offer interstate security. This precarious system unravelled on June 28, 1914, with the assassination of the Austrian archduke Ferdinand and his wife by a Bosnian patriot. The Austro-Hungarian government, suspecting Serbian involvement, issued an ultimatum; the Serbians rejected it immediately; Austro-Hungary mobilized for war; the Russians, as protectors of the fellow Slavs, also mobilized for war against Austria-Hungary; the Germans followed as allies of Austria-Hungary, declared war on France as Russia's ally, and advanced through Belgium; Britain, guaranteeing Belgium neutrality, declared war on Germany on August 4. In a little over five weeks the major powers of Europe were involved in massive and bloody struggle.

Canada, as part of the British empire, immediately raised an expeditionary force to be sent to France. Canadian troops, at first part of the British army, took part in most of the major battles on the western front between 1914 and 1918. By 1918 the Canadians had become a complete army organization. Canada sent over 400,000 men to Europe and during the course of the war suffered some 27 percent casualties.

The United States was drawn slowly but surely into the war. The most important issue related to the rights of neutral shipping. The Wilson administration insisted on the application of neutrality rights for U.S. ships to traverse the Atlantic and continue its trade with both the Central and Allied powers. In reality, though perhaps the United States was legally neutral, the U.S. trade with Britain was ten times that of its trade with Germany. In attempts to stop the resupply of the British, German U-boats sunk ships with Americans aboard throughout the period of hostilities from 1914, the most famous of which were perhaps the *Lusitania* and the *Sussex*. The former, though ostensibly neutral, carried munitions bound for Britain. Nevertheless, without this information being publicly available, U.S. public opinion was outraged. By the spring of 1917, Germany resumed its use of U-boats, which was one of the most direct causes of U.S. involvement.

Also by 1917, President Woodrow Wilson and his cabinet realized that the United States could not have an effect on the future ideological shape of the world if it were not included in the peace talks at the end of the war. The United

States declared war on the Central powers in April 1917, after three years of war in Europe. The U.S. forces began to arrive during the summer of 1917, but the American Expeditionary Force (AEF), which fought only as an Associated power, not an Ally, did not see its first major action until the final German offensive in the spring of 1918. The U.S. productive capacity made a considerable difference. This was especially important as the front lines in the west had not moved significantly for months, and in the east, after the Bolshevik revolution of October 1917, the new Russian state pulled its troops out of the war.

Having failed in the final offensive, the Germans began to retreat, and, with millions of casualties, the Armistice in the west was finally signed on November 11, 1918. Canada sat with the United States at the peace conference of Versailles in 1918–1919. President Woodrow Wilson intended to make the world "safe for Democracy" and to promote "self-determination" throughout the European world. His Fourteen Points, containing many of the principles of U.S. foreign policy, and his idea to create a League of Nations, which through collective security would supposedly prevent future wars, initially became the basis of the peace talks. Though Wilson largely failed at Versailles, and the U.S. Senate rejected membership in the League, Wilsonian ideals ultimately had a profound impact on the course of twentieth-century history.

DEPRESSION TO NEW DEAL

On the bread line, a charity feeds the unemployed, New York, February 1932.

The Great Crash, Tuesday, October 29, 1929: a then-record sixteen million shares were sold on the Wall Street stock market, at ever decreasing prices. On the previous Thursday, thirteen million shares had been sold, with $11 billion wiped off share values, but there had been sounds of reassurance from government experts and major business, as there had been all summer before, and it had seemed the slide had been halted. Unfortunately, there was little real foundation for the reassurance, and anxiety soon reasserted itself.

Investors had a right to be worried. Share prices had continued to rise as production had declined. Speculation was firing the stock market, but America's working population was seeing little of the money trickle down in the form of wages, so demand for the goods made by the companies in which people were buying shares was not strong. If the foundations of this boom were weak, so was the security of the money being invested. Many investors were trading "on the margin." That is, they were borrowing money in order to invest. All very well in a rapidly rising market, this becomes a problem when the market falls, and the investors find their stock falling and their loans called in.

Within two weeks, up to $50 billion had been wiped from the value of shares. President Hoover and his Republican administration remained hopeful that confidence would return, and that the American economy would reestablish the upward trend that had typified recent decades. With unemployment at four million and rising, some public investment in public buildings and roads was initiated, but the government remained committed to the view that relief of economic problems was an individual and local responsibility, rather than that of national government.

An outburst of international protectionism served to limit the trade that might have stimulated industrial output. At the same time, public mistrust of financial institutions led many to want their savings in cash.

By the time of the 1932 elections, unemployment had reached thirteen million. The Democrats, promising "a new deal for the American people," took control of Congress and the presidency. While it is not clear that the new administration had an understanding of what policies might work, President Franklin D. Roosevelt realized the need for dramatic and rapid action to restore confidence. A four-day bank holiday was declared, Congress was called into special session, and the Emergency Banking Act was passed on its first day. There followed a period of intense government activity, when legislation was passed to increase the regulation of industry, food production, price levels, financial institutions, and labor relations. Much of this legislation provided government-financed employment, such as through the Civilian Conservation Corps and the Public Works Administration.

Many saw this legislation as radical, and legal challenges were launched. The Supreme Court proved sympathetic to these challenges and in 1935 and 1936 declared major parts of the New Deal unconstitutional. Roosevelt was returned to the White House in November 1936 with overwhelming public support, and responded to the legal setbacks with a plan to add new seats to the Supreme

Court. This time his plans were too radical to be passed, but a change of opinion by a Supreme Court justice, followed by retirements of others, meant that a more sympathetic judiciary was soon in place, and the legislation of the Second New Deal was soon under way.

In Canada, efforts to relieve a similar economic crisis were initiated; 162 work camps were established, housing some 170,000 men. Welfare, usually a provincial undertaking, was taken over by the dominion's government as local administrations fell into financial crisis.

Not until 1937 were American production levels back to 1929 standards, and that was not to last long, with a slump in the late part of that year. Public support for Roosevelt began to wane, but the approach of war provided a reason to rally around the leader, and a stimulus for the American economy. As the Depression slipped away, America was left with a greatly extended sphere of government intervention, the core of a welfare state, and a political system aligned for a generation to come on the partisan political battles that came of the the Great Wall Street Crash.

VOTE, 1928

Hoover (Republican)

Smith (Democrat)

VOTE, 1932

Roosevelt (Democrat)

Hoover (Republican)

VOTE, 1936

Roosevelt (Democrat)

Landon (Republican)

• airport constructed or approved by Works Progress Administration

0   300 km

0   300 miles

115

THE COMING OF WAR

Despite the devastating attack on Pearl Harbor, the long-term effectiveness of the U.S. fleet was not impaired. Its three carriers were not in port and most of the ships sunk were later raised and rebuilt.

The rise of Germany under its new leader, Adolf Hitler, had been rapid. By 1939 the Treaty of Versailles had been cast aside. Germany had rearmed, occupied the Rhineland, united with Austria, swallowed Czechoslovakia, and invaded Poland on September 1, 1939. The latter was the final act that brought Britain and its empire including Canada along with France into war with Germany.

Japan looked on, having drawn up its own plans for expansion. With the major European colonial powers at war, their territories in Asia lay exposed, there remained just the United States to deal with. Though the United States did not officially enter the Second World War until after the attack on Pearl Harbor, President Roosevelt had taken the executive decision to move U.S. naval power farther east across the Atlantic between 1939 and 1941. The U.S. Navy was protecting convoys of British ships that were collecting supplies under the Lend-Lease agreement of 1941. By April 1941, the U.S. was patrolling for German submarines midway across the Atlantic. Roosevelt had reasoned that the nation or Congress was not ready for the role of protecting British ships with the possibility of war. The Isolationist sentiment was still powerful.

During October and November 1941, Secretary of State Cordell Hull negotiated with the Japanese, seeking concessions to avoid a war in the Pacific, which

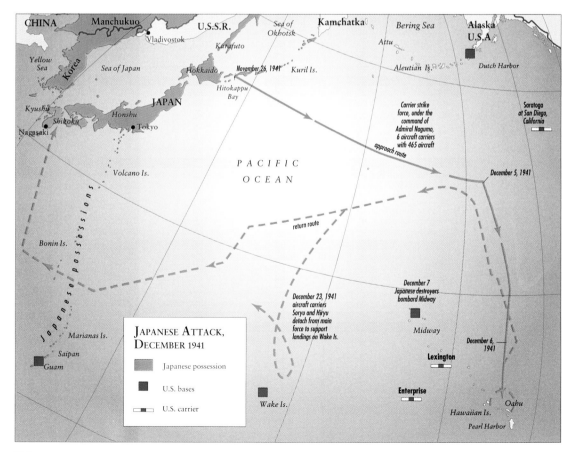

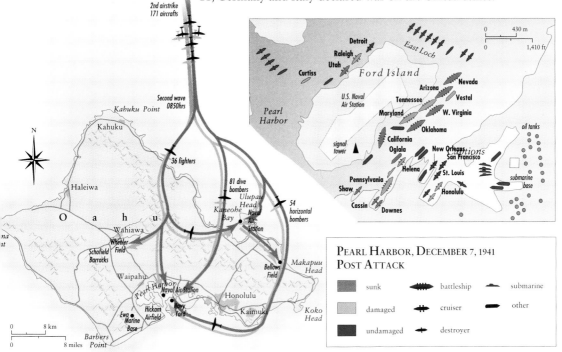

PEARL HARBOR,
DECEMBER 7, 1941

1st airstrike
189 aircrafts

U.S. military leaders did not want until their forces were strengthened. Hull demanded that Japan cease its aggression against China and Southeast Asia, after which the United States would resume the oil supply to Japan; the United States also wanted Japan to withdraw from China and respect the Open Door policies for the region. Japan was willing to consider several issues, but not to withdraw totally from China after ten years of occupation. By December 1941, war with Japan was considered inevitable.

Hideki Tojo's government ordered an attack on the United States in late November after the talks broke down. The United States had broken the Japanese codes and read the intercepts before beginning negotiations with the Japanese ambassador. On November 27, Washington informed commanders at Pearl Harbor that the Japanese would attack within days, but the location could not be confirmed.

By December 6, the Japanese fleet of six aircraft carriers and escorts had reached a position 250 miles north of Hawaii. At dawn the following day, they struck at the U.S. fleet, leaving 3,600 U.S. casualties, killed and wounded, and the fleet devastated.

The following day, Roosevelt addressed a Joint Session of Congress, declaring December 7, 1941, as "a date which will live in infamy." The United States and Britain declared war on Japan. Within days, the United States overcame its reluctance to use force in the Atlantic. On December 11, Germany and Italy declared war on the United States.

First wave
0740hrs

Kahuku Point
54 dive bombers
45 fighters
Kahuku

PACIFIC
OCEAN

Haleiwa

Ulupau
Head
Kaneohe
Bay Naval Air Station

O   a   h   u

Wahiawa
Wheeler
Field
Schofield
Barracks

aena
int

40 torpedo
bombers

Makapuu
Head

Bellows
Field

Waipahu   Pearl Harbor
Naval Air Station

Honolulu

50 horizontal
bombers

Ewa
Marine
Base

Navy
Yard

Hickam
Airfield

Kaimuki   Koko
Head

Diamond
Head

Barbers
Point

0   8 km

0   8 miles

2nd airstrike
171 aircrafts

Second wave
0850hrs

Kahuku Point
Kahuku

N

36 fighters

81 dive
bombers
Ulupau
Head
Kaneohe Naval
Bay   Air
Station

54
horizontal
bombers

Haleiwa

O   a   h   u

na
it

Wahiawa
Wheeler
Field
Schofield
Barracks

Bellows
Field

Makapuu
Head

Waipahu

Pearl Harbor
Naval Air Station

Honolulu

Ewa
Marine
Base

Hickam
Airfield

Navy
Yard

Kaimuki   Koko
Head

Barbers
Point

0   8 km

0   8 miles

Detroit
Raleigh
Utah
Curtiss

East Loch

Ford Island

Nevada
Arizona   Vestal
U.S. Naval
Air Station

Tennessee
Maryland

W. Virginia

Oklahoma

Pearl
Harbor

oil tanks

signal
tower

California
Oglala

New Orleans
San Francisco

Helena   St. Louis

submarine
base

Pennsylvania

Shaw

Honolulu

Cassin

Downes

0   430 m

0   1,410 ft

PEARL HARBOR, DECEMBER 7, 1941
POST ATTACK

sunk	battleship	submarine
damaged	cruiser	other
undamaged	destroyer	

WORLD WAR II IN EUROPE, 1942–1945

Winston Churchill, President Franklin D. Roosevelt, and Josef Stalin, Yalta, 1945.

"The work, my friend, is peace. More than an end of this war—an end to the beginnings of all wars."
Franklin D. Roosevelt, intended address for Jefferson Day, April 13, 1945

Though the United States had been attacked first in the Pacific and fought the Japanese from 1941 to 1945, their primary concerns were in the Atlantic and Europe. Hitler's Germany represented the core of the threat to U.S. interests and potentially a stupendous strategic prize, given that it had risen to world prominence twice already (after unification in the 1870s, and after World War I), and would rise as an industrial and commercial power again after World War II.

Soviet forces under Stalin bore the brunt of the German attack in Operation Barbarossa in June 1941, and continued to do the bulk of the fighting on the eastern front, suffering horrendous casualties. Stalin expected the Western allies to deliver on their promise of opening a second front in Western Europe. Instead, the United States under the command of Dwight Eisenhower, launched Operation Torch across North Africa in November 1942. As the U.S. forces moved east through Morocco and Algeria, the British moved west from Egypt, defeating the German forces in North Africa initially sent there in April 1941 to assist their Italian allies. The United States with British and Canadian forces then invaded Sicily in July and August 1943, moving on to Italy in September. Though the Italians capitulated and their fascist leader Mussolini was overthrown, German troops continued to resist the Allied forces. Ultimately, Rome fell in early June 1944, two days before the Allies landed in Northern France. This strategy allowed the Soviets to gain territories in Europe, from which they were reluctant to retreat after the war.

The Allied invasion of French Normandy began on June 6 (D-Day), in Operation Overlord. Over 12,000 aircraft and 6,500 ships brought thousands of troops ashore under heavy German resistance. Casualties were considerable. The actual perimeter established was not as extensive as the Allies originally planned, but was consolidated within weeks. Through July and August, Allied troops moved south and east through France. Paris was liberated by French and U.S. troops on August 25, and by the end of September, most of France and Belgium had been liberated from German occupation. British and Canadian troops entered Brussels on September 5.

In February 1945, the "Big Three," Stalin, President Roosevelt, and British Prime Minister Churchill, met at Yalta on the coast of the Black Sea, to plan the unconditional surrender it would demand from Germany and to craft the Declaration of a Liberated Europe. The simmering tensions that existed in earlier conferences could not be resolved conclusively. U.S. troops crossed the Rhine River in March and moved by mid-April on to the Elbe River, where by prior agreement they would stop, allowing Soviet forces to take Berlin by June 2, two days after Hitler committed suicide. A week later, German forces surrendered to Eisenhower, and Russian commander Von Keitel surrendered to Field Marshal Zhukov on May 8, 1945. Victory in Europe had been achieved. The war in Asia continued for another three months.

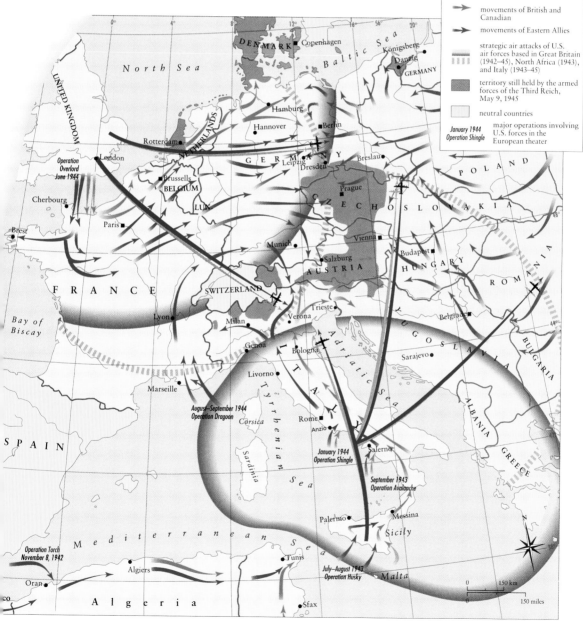

THE LIBERATION OF EUROPE

main movements of U.S. armed forces in North African and European campaigns, 1942–45

movements of British and Canadian

movements of Eastern Allies

strategic air attacks of U.S. air forces based in Great Britain (1942–45), North Africa (1943), and Italy (1943–45)

territory still held by the armed forces of the Third Reich, May 9, 1945

neutral countries

January 1944 Operation Shingle — major operations involving U.S. forces in the European theater

World War II in the Pacific, 1943–45

By 1942, the Japanese empire extended over a considerable portion of the Pacific throughout Southeast Asia, having driving the British from Malaya, the Dutch from the East Indies, and the Americans from the Philippines. By June 1942, the United States began its counterattack after the failed Japanese attempt to capture the Midway Islands. The U.S. victory there demonstrated the vitality of air power, and provided a morale boost to U.S. forces after Pearl Harbor.

Therafter, a slow but steady Allied attack began on the Japanese navy and the outposts of the Japanese empire. In August 1942, the United States launched its invasion of Guadalcanal, losing many lives in the first Pacific offensive. From then on the combined strength of the navy and ground troops continued the strategy of island-hopping, reaching New Guinea, the Dutch East Indies, and the Philippines by June 1944. The recapture of the Philippine Islands was a lengthy operation, the remnants of Japanese forces holding out until September 1945. In the campaigns of the south Pacific, the U.S. forces operated alongside Australian, New Zealand, and even a small Mexican aviation unit. Meanwhile, in a long and bloody campaign, British and Indian forces had retaken Burma by August 1945.

In February 1945, landings began on Iwo Jima. The struggle to capture this strategically important island lasted over a month, with Japanese troops fighting for every inch of ground. The U.S. air force began operations, bombing the Japanese homeland in April; U.S. heavy bombers could now be escorted by fighters. On April 1, U.S. marines landed on Okinawa, and the final major engagement of the Pacific was under way. Ultimately the Japanese would lose 110,000 killed in the fighting, and only 7,000 were taken alive. The United States lost 12,281, including their commanding general; things did not bode well for the projected landings on Japan.

During the last of the wartime conferences between the Allies in Potsdam, apart from the

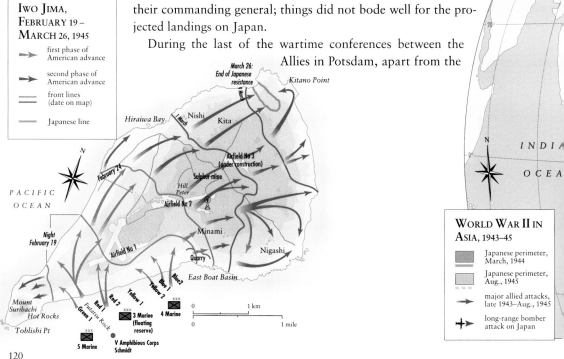

Iwo Jima, February 19 – March 26, 1945

- first phase of American advance
- second phase of American advance
- front lines (date on map)
- Japanese line

March 26: End of Japanese resistance

Kitano Point

Hiraiwa Bay · Nishi · Kita

Airfield No 3 (under construction)

Sulphur mine

Hill Peter

Airfield No 2

Minami

Nigashi

PACIFIC OCEAN

Night February 19

Airfield No 1

Quarry

East Boat Basin

Red 1 · Red 2 · Yellow 1 · Yellow 2 · Blue 1 · Blue 2

3 Marine (floating reserve) · 4 Marine

Mount Suribachi · Hot Rocks · Futatsu Rock · Green 1

Toblishi Pt

5 Marine · V Amphibious Corps Schmidt

0 — 1 km
0 — 1 mile

World War II in Asia, 1943–45

- Japanese perimeter, March, 1944
- Japanese perimeter, Aug., 1945
- major allied attacks, late 1943–Aug., 1945
- long-range bomber attack on Japan

INDIA

OCEA

German problem, the terms of surrender were debated. Japan was required to surrender unconditionally. Russia had promised to enter the war three months after Victory in Europe Day. During the Potsdam Conference, President Truman received news of the successful test of the atomic bomb in the deserts of New Mexico at Alamagordo. Within weeks, two nuclear bombs were dropped—one on Hiroshima (August 6) and one on Nagasaki (August 9). Between these two dates the Soviets had entered the war, sweeping rapidly through Manchuria. Figures of direct casualties diverge widely. In Hiroshima, 80,000 died that day, with about 60,000 further deaths following in the aftermath. In Nagasaki a further 65,000 people were killed. Japan surrendered to the United States on August 14, 1945. World War II was over.

① June 1942 – July 1943
Operation Cartwheel. Allied forces advance.

② November 1943 – September 1944
U.S. drive through central Pacific.

③ February – June, 1944
Unsuccessful Japanese invasion of India.

④ October 19–21, 1944
Battle of the Philippine Sea. U.S. Task Force 58 destroys Japanese Mobile Fleet.

⑤ October 20, 1944
U.S. forces land in Philippines.

⑥ Nov. 24, 1944
20th Air Force begins air attack on Japan from Island bases.

⑦ November 1944
British offensive into Burma.

⑧ February 19 – March 26, 1945
U.S. captures Iwo Jima
April 1 – June 1945
U.S. land and capture Okinawa.

⑨ April – June 1945
Chinese offensives.

⑩ August 9, 1945
Soviet offensive begins.

⑪ August 6 and August 9, 1945
U.S. nuclear attacks on Japan.

PART VI: SUPERPOWER

With the backing of the United Nations Security Council, U.S. soldiers found themselves committed to the defense of South Korea. They were later joined by other UN forces that included Canadian ground and air forces.

Following the Second World War, the victorious powers of the Grand Alliance soon moved toward greater antagonism. This was partly a result of severe disagreement on the postwar division of Europe and the future of Germany, and partly a result of the strategies and diplomacy employed during the war. It also heightened the animosity between the United States and the Soviet Union since the latter's formation, as well as ideological differences with the Bolsheviks since the Russian revolution. The hostility that emerged centered on Europe in the initial postwar years, but soon widened to include Asia, with the most significant conflicts taking place in Korea and Vietnam. Traditionally the "Cold War" referred to a bipolar confrontation primarily involving the antagonism between the two Superpowers. Hans Morgenthau wrote in 1954 that "the international situation is reduced to the primitive spectacle of two giants eyeing each other with watchful suspicion." Others drew the analogy of a scorpion and a tarantula in a bottle poised for a fight to the death. But the very term "Cold War" implied that direct conflict did not take place. There were mutual recriminations, ideological battles, propaganda, obstruction, threats, and covert action, but little direct physical action.

As the Cold War widened to find expression in various regional conflicts, from Korea in the early 1950s to the so-called first post–Cold War conflict in the Persian Gulf, the Superpowers had been involved in a multitude of regional conflicts around the globe. These conflicts were not primarily a result of the traditional idea of the Cold War hostilities. They often had much longer and more important local or regional causes, to be sure, and they were significantly exacerbated by the Superpowers, creating hot wars resulting in an estimated twenty-five to thirty million deaths.

From the immediate postwar period, the United States, and to a lesser extent Canada, demonstrated enormous economic power in support of the various reconstruction programs in both Europe and Japan. Though of course there was an element of self-interest in the programs (creating a market for exports, exercising control in Japan and hegemony in Europe), the United States and Canada were the only major powers to emerge from the conflict relatively unscathed. The U.S. forces were technically superior to those of the Soviet Union, and the United States maintained a monopoly on nuclear weapons for a number of years.

Following the delineation of postwar Europe—the United States and its allies controlling the west, the Soviet Union the east—by the early 1950s the United States initiated a significant arms buildup. By the time President Eisenhower left office, he warned the country about the potential power of the

"Military Industrial Complex." Such power was deemed necessary to "contain" a supposedly expanding Soviet Union in both Europe and the Third World. Even though the intense hostility waned after the death of Stalin in 1953, until the Cuban Missile Crisis (1962) the Superpowers engaged in an almost continuous arms race. In search of a first-strike capability, the Superpowers threatened each other with Mutually Assured Destruction (MAD), and engaged in a strategy of deterrence.

Because the prospect of direct nuclear conflict was undesirable, the Superpower hostility found expression in the competition for greater influence in the Third World. In these areas the United States sought to roll back what it perceived as the extension of Soviet power, though in many cases Washington

Global commitment. Here, United States armed forces prepare for a training exercise in West Germany, October 1962.

often confused or labeled indigenous or nationalist forces as "Communist" to justify their policies. During the 1950s the United States deployed its power in Iran and Guatemala against local forces trying to gain control of their resources. Later still, Washington moved against two of its ostensible allies during the Suez crisis, when Egypt nationalized the Suez Canal in 1956. Britain and France saw this as a threat to their strategic link connecting them directly to their far-eastern colonial possessions. Britain, France, and Israel attacked Egypt, intending to sieze control of the canal zone. Within a few days the United States had intervened and put an end to this operation.

In many ways, the 1950s were the apotheosis of U.S. power. In terms of its economy, its military power, the appeal of its ideology, and the impact of its culture, the United States was definitively a Superpower and the center of the Western system. However, by the end of the decade the formation of the European Economic Community in 1957 began to challenge U.S. economic supremacy, competition in the Third World intensified, and by the early 1960s the Soviet Union tested the U.S. resolve during the Cuban Missile Crisis.

With the continued intensification of the civil war in Vietnam, Washington became more and more enmeshed, significantly escalating the war from the mid-1960s onward. The costs to the Vietnamese were horrendous. The costs to the United States as a Superpower were significant. The United States no longer maintained the flexibility of its power; the economy suffered considerably; the influence and credibility of the United States declined; and the United States lost its assumed prestige, and ultimately had to withdraw from Vietnam and devalue its currency. In all, over 58,000 U.S. personnel lost their lives.

The costs of maintaining a Cold War economy had become so acute by the early 1970s that the United States could no longer afford to "pay any price" to assure the survival of liberty, as President Kennedy had urged them to do in 1961. An era of détente, or a relaxation of tensions, was initiated between the United States and the Soviet Union in the late 1960s and prevailed through to the late 1970s. During this period, the two countries reached significant agreements on arms control, economic exchange, and cultural ties. Both Superpowers consolidated their ties with the other world powers. Washington took advantage of the Sino-Soviet split to open relations with Beijing in 1972, and Washington became increasingly wary of its allies' economic agenda. In many ways the Cold War construct broke down. The Middle Eastern–dominated oil cartel (OPEC) explicitly challenged the West over control of their resources in 1973, and throughout most of the decade, Third World revolutions, though not necessarily linked to Moscow, gave the appearance of U.S. weakness. The Carter administration's attempt to extricate the United States from what he called its "inordinate fear of Communism" further exacerbated the perception of a Superpower in retreat.

Following the malaise of the 1970s, and the perceived Soviet gains, the Reagan administration (1981–1989) initiated a tough response. It dramatically increased spending on the arms race, initiating the Strategic Defense Initiative (SDI) in 1983, threatened to confine the Soviet Union to the "ash heap" of history, and took much more direct action against revolutionary states in the Third World. By mid-decade Washington proved more conciliatory after Mikhail Gorbachev came to power. A series of Superpower summits were initiated in 1985 on an almost annual basis. By 1987, the Soviet Union began pulling its support and troops out of several Third World countries; by 1989, its power collapsed in Eastern Europe; and by 1991, the Soviet Union itself disintegrated.

The costs of operating as a Superpower, with a significant proportion of the annual budget given over to defense, eventually caught up with the United States. By 1985, it had become a debtor nation, and soon moved into the position of becoming the largest debtor nation in the world. Nevertheless, as the Cold War ended, analysts talked about the "unipopular moment" when the United States was the only Superpower, while others, referring to the relative decline in U.S. power, argued that the United States would have to become used to being a "great" power, but one among many. Still, during the Gulf War of 1991, the United States reestablished its mobility of power to devastating effect.

> "I urge you to beware the temptation of pride—the temptation blithely to declare yourselves above it all and label both sides equally at fault, to ignore the facts of history and the aggressive impulses of an evil empire."
> *Ronald Reagan,*
> March 1983

The cutting edge of technology helps the United States maintain its position as the world superpower. The Stealth fighter, left, almost impossible to track on radar, is just part of that technology.

POSTWAR WORLD AND COLD WAR

By the time the war in Europe ended, the Soviet Army had occupied large sections of Eastern Europe, largely as a result of the Western Allies' inability to open up a second front until 1944, choosing instead to initiate their invasion of mainland Europe through North Africa in 1942 and through Italy in 1943.

When Churchill, Roosevelt, and Stalin met at Yalta in February 1945 to plan the postwar order, the Soviet presence in Eastern Europe was very much a reality that could not be ignored or wished away. The Declaration on a Liberated Europe required free elections for all countries, though Roosevelt had realized that there was not much prospect for this in the Eastern countries. Critics have since charged Roosevelt with selling out the East and betraying the ideals for which the United States entered the war as the "Arsenal of Democracy."

The two major postwar powers, the United States and the Soviet Union, vied for control in their respective spheres of influence. Germany was initially divided among the four powers, but soon the U.S., British, and French sections joined to ultimately divide the nation into what became the Federal Republic of Germany and the Democratic Republic of Germany. Communist governments were soon installed in Eastern Europe.

In the West the United States sought to exert its influence through economic assistance and, in 1948, the Marshall Plan provided sixteen nations with $13 billion over a period of four years. In the political sphere, U.S. policy planner George Kennan initiated a strategy of containment, which became the basis of the Truman Doctrine in April 1947.

The Cold War in Europe remained tense and hostile, with several crises erupting around Berlin. Of particular note is the Soviet blockade of Berlin during 1948 and 1949, during which the Western air forces airlifted supplies to the city for almost a year. The city remained a central point in the Cold War. In 1961, Premier Nikita Khrushchev ordered the erection of the Berlin Wall, dividing the city to prevent the escape of East Germans to the West.

SOVIET AND AMERICAN BLOCS, 1960–89

Counterforce V MAD (Mutually Assumed Destruction)

■ U.S. and allies

□ USSR and allies

⏐ Soviet missile sites

■ principal Soviet military airfield

⏐ U.S. ICBM bases (5,500-mile range)

■ U.S. heavy bomber bases

▲ U.S. nuclear and other major bases

⬛ strategic U.S. fleets

◆▶ points of conflict during the Cold War

Whether through design or misunderstanding, the system of a divided Europe and then a divided world remained for the best part of forty-five years of Cold War, neither peaceful nor in a state of direct war. The prospects of a protracted war between the United States and the Soviet Union became less likely after 1949, when both powers had exploded nuclear bombs. Though at this point the Soviets did not have the ability to deliver the bombs, soon an arms race began between the powers, which, if unleashed, would have brought about their mutual destruction. Despite the frozen nature of the conflict at the "center" in Europe, proxy warfare occurred in the Third World.

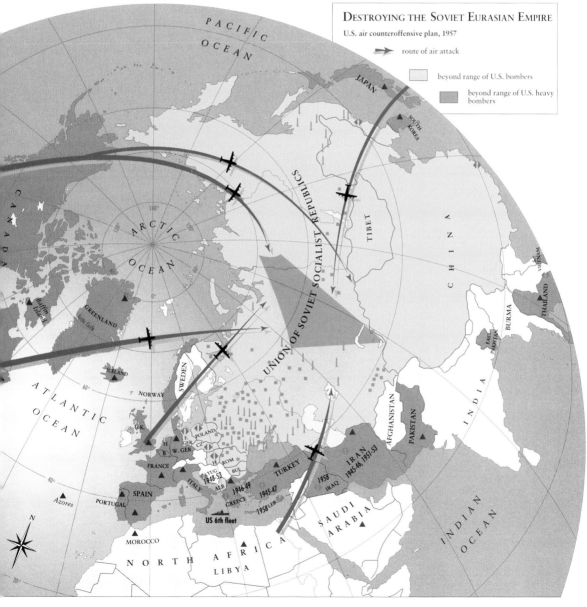

DESTROYING THE SOVIET EURASIAN EMPIRE

U.S. air counteroffensive plan, 1957

route of air attack

beyond range of U.S. bombers

beyond range of U.S. heavy bombers

127

KOREA

Korea was divided between the victorious powers following the Japanese surrender in August 1945. By 1948, the two parts of Korea had formed into independent countries, though politicians on both sides of the divide sought reunification on very different terms. North Korea with its capital at P'yongyang was ruled by Marshall Kim il Sung, whose Democratic People's Republic was backed by the Soviet Union. In the South, the Rhee government was backed by the United States.

After the Rhee government refused to abide by the results of a vote in South Korea to seek unification even if necessary on North Korean terms, the ongoing border skirmishes turned into outright invasion by the North Koreans. Though the U.S. secretary of state, Dean Acheson, had earlier placed South Korea beyond the range of the agreed U.S. Defensive Perimeter in January 1950, once the actual attack came, the stakes were not just military but also political. As the Cold War was then presented and perhaps perceived as a stalemate, such an invasion, if it had not resulted in a U.S. response, would appear to be an advance for the Soviet Union, undermining U.S. credibility and commitment and bringing into question the "containment" policy in Asia.

Once the North Koreans had crossed the 38th parallel, their advance to Seoul took three days. The North Koreans continued down the peninsula until they met U.S. resistance in the southeast around Pusan in September 1950. Sixteen nations sent their troops to Korea as part of the UN action to resist the invasion, though the United States provided the most decisive military contribution.

By mid-September, General Douglas MacArthur launched an attack to the southwest of Seoul at Inch'on. Within the week, UN forces had captured Seoul and severed the North Koreans' supply lines to the south, forcing their retreat back to the North.

By the end of September, U.S. president Truman permitted MacArthur to pursue the North Koreans across the 38th parallel with the instructions to destroy the North Korean armed forces. MacArthur's advance was equally swift, leading to the capture of P'yongyang by October 20. Despite the earlier Chinese warning that they considered the U.S. advance dangerous to their security, by late October, UN forces had advanced to within 100 miles of the Yalu River, the border between China and North Korea.

NORTH KOREAN OFFENSIVE, JUNE–AUGUST 1950

— frontline

held by U.S. forces, September 10

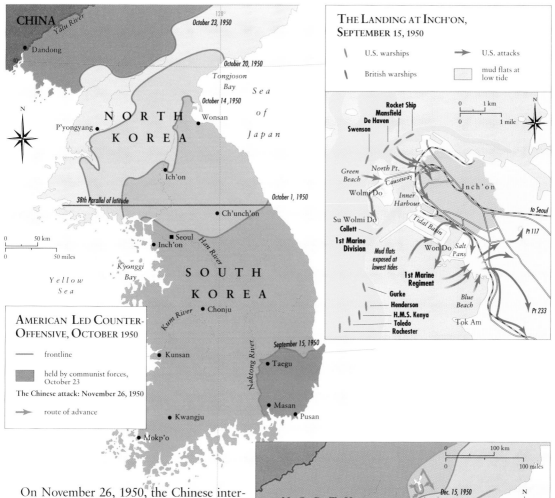

CHINA

Yalu River

October 23, 1950

• Dandong

October 20, 1950

Tongjoson
Bay

October 14, 1950

Sea

of

Japan

NORTH

KOREA

• P'yongyang   • Wonsan

N

• Ich'on

38th Parallel of latitude   October 1, 1950

• Ch'unch'on

0   50 km

0   50 miles

Han River

Kyonggi
Bay

• Seoul
• Inch'on

Yellow
Sea

SOUTH

KOREA

Kum River   • Chonju

September 15, 1950

Naktong River

• Taegu

• Kunsan

AMERICAN LED COUNTER-OFFENSIVE, OCTOBER 1950

— frontline

held by communist forces, October 23

The Chinese attack: November 26, 1950

→ route of advance

• Masan

• Kwangju   Pusan

• Mokp'o

THE LANDING AT INCH'ON, SEPTEMBER 15, 1950

\ U.S. warships   → U.S. attacks

\ British warships   ☐ mud flats at low tide

Rocket Ship
Mansfield
De Haven
Swenson

0   1 km

0   1 mile

N

Green
Beach   North Pt.

Causeway   Inch'on

Wolmi Do

Su Wolmi Do   Inner
Harbour

Collett

Tidal Basin   to Seoul

**1st Marine
Division**   Won Do   Salt
Pans   Pt 117

Mud flats
exposed at
lowest tides

**1st Marine
Regiment**

Gurke   Blue
Henderson   Beach   Pt 233

H.M.S. Kenya

Toledo   Tok Am

Rochester

On November 26, 1950, the Chinese intervened to destroy MacArthur's position and the threat U.S. troops posed to Chinese security. The Chinese forced the U.S. and UN troops to retreat swiftly back down the peninsula. By the spring of 1951 the war stood about where it had begun. For the next two years giant conventional armies slaughtered each other along a shifting front in the middle of the peninsula, until an armistice, on July 27, 1953. Meanwhile, Truman had sacked MacArthur; the general's stinging criticism of Truman contributed to his decision not to run for the presidency in 1952, and it was left to the newly elected President Eisenhower to bring the war to an end.

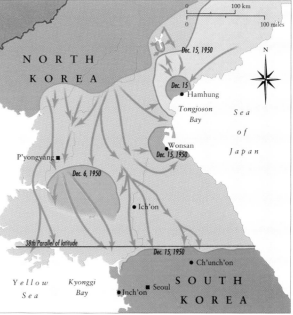

0   100 km

0   100 miles

Dec. 15, 1950

NORTH

KOREA

N

Dec. 15
• Hamhung

Tongjoson
Bay   Sea

of

• Wonsan   Japan

P'yongyang ■   Dec. 15, 1950

Dec. 6, 1950

• Ich'on

38th Parallel of latitude   Dec. 15, 1950

• Ch'unch'on

Yellow   Kyonggi   SOUTH
Sea   Bay   Inch'on ■ Seoul   KOREA

VIETNAM

One of the most dangerous tasks of the war, an air landing in enemy territory, here launched by part of the 1st Cavalry Division, March 1966.

Since the 1860s, the three provinces of Vietnam—Tonkin, Annam, and Cochin—had become important colonies for the French. Though the area was lost to the Japanese during the Second World War, France insisted on regaining control of the area in 1945. Vietnamese nationalist leader Ho Chi Minh, founder of the Indochinese Communist Party, had long sought independence for Vietnam. At Versailles in 1918–1919, he petitioned U.S. President Woodrow Wilson to no avail, and during the Second World War, Ho worked for U.S. intelligence against the Japanese. In 1945, U.S. agents helped Ho write a declaration of independence for Vietnam. The Declaration of Vietnamese Independence was largely modeled on the U.S. Declaration.

By 1946, the French had returned and protracted warfare ensued between the French and the Vietnamese Independence League or Vietminh, whose strongholds were in the North. Over the following decade, the French lost close to 70,000 troops. During the period, the United States was financing more than 50 percent of the French military expenditures. In 1954, an ingenious military assault, devised by Vietminh general Vo Nguyen Giap, decisively defeated the French at Dien Bien Phu. Washington considered the use of nuclear weapons to save the French position, but Eisenhower objected to the scheme. The negotiations held in Geneva in the summer of 1954 divided the country at the 17th parallel, with Vietminh control in the North and the U.S.-backed government of Ngo Dinh Diem, under the emperor Bao Dai, in the South. Elections were to be held in 1956 to determine who would rule the entire country. After the CIA estimated that Ho would easily win the elections, Diem decided to hold separate elections in the South, taking a fraudulent 98.2 percent of the vote.

There has always been disagreement on the reasons why the United States became involved in Vietnam. While some cite the need to contain the advance of Communism, others contend that Ho's revolution, though Communist, was more nationalist and not under the direction of the Soviet Union or China. Still others contend that Vietnam was, in the early postwar period, a vital component of the French economy, and later a vital component of the Japanese economic system. It was in the U.S. interest not to see any of these key allies' economies suffer during the Cold War.

Though U.S. President John F. Kennedy was advised by French President Charles De Gaulle not to become involved in Vietnam, Kennedy had also pledged to "pay any price" to "ensure the survival and success of liberty." Thus, to some extent, U.S. credibility was at stake in Vietnam, should there be any further Communist advances. President Eisenhower had compared the region to a row of dominoes falling to Communism. The analogy became politically useful, and was often inappropriately repeated thereafter. Kennedy introduced 16,000 U.S. "advisors" into Vietnam, describing the country as the "cornerstone of the Free World."

After the Battle of Ap Bac in January 1963, the Vietcong, the name given to the Vietnamese Communists in the South, demonstrated their formidable fighting ability and the ineptitude of the ARVN, the South Vietnamese Army. Most U.S. generals concluded that the South could survive in the Western camp only if the United States took over the military operations. For months, the Kennedy and then the Johnson administrations searched for a way to introduce greater numbers of U.S. troops. The solution came in August 1964, in what later became known as the Gulf of Tonkin incident. On August 2, the U.S. destroyer *Maddox* came under fire and retaliated. Two days later, the episode was supposedly repeated, though it is largely thought to be fictitious, and within days Congress passed the Gulf of Tonkin Resolution by 411 to 0, giving President Lyndon Johnson a virtual blank check to use force.

Johnson retaliated for the Tonkin incident by bombing coastal installations in North Vietnam. From there on, the U.S. involvement progressively increased. First the U.S. troops were sent to secure the U.S. enclaves. In March 1965, marines landed at Da Nang to secure their air bases. General William Westmoreland sought further engagement and commenced the process of "search and destroy" missions in a war of attrition against the Vietcong. Westmoreland initiated the repeated requests for additional U.S. troops, which at the height of the war amounted to over half a million active in Vietnam. Simultaneously, the Vietcong had launched offensives against the U.S. air

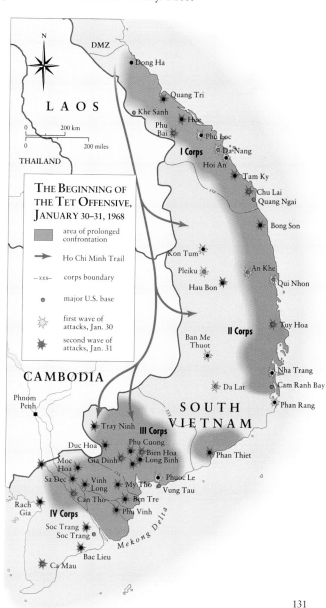

THE BEGINNING OF THE TET OFFENSIVE, JANUARY 30–31, 1968

area of prolonged confrontation

Ho Chi Minh Trail

corps boundary

major U.S. base

first wave of attacks, Jan. 30

second wave of attacks, Jan. 31

bases, most importantly at Pleiku in February 1965. The retaliation or aerial bombard-ment, ordered by Johnson, soon became "Operation Rolling Thunder." More bombs were dropped in Vietnam than in all of history hitherto. Initially, Johnson was reluctant to bomb deep into North Vietnam for fear that the Chinese or the Soviets might retaliate. Though frustrated with the lack

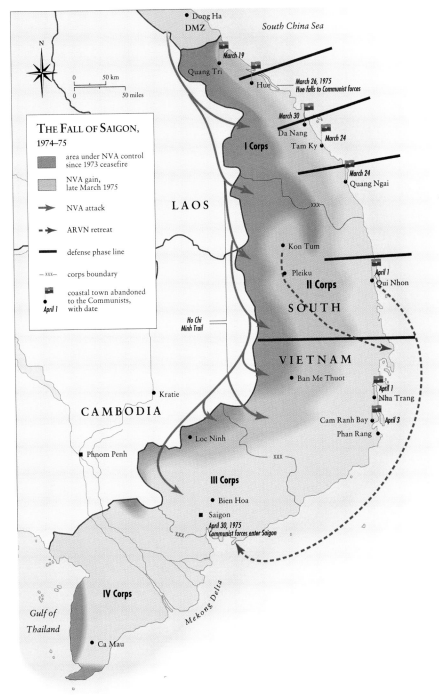

THE FALL OF SAIGON, 1974–75

area under NVA control since 1973 ceasefire

NVA gain, late March 1975

NVA attack

ARVN retreat

defense phase line

—xxx— corps boundary

coastal town abandoned to the Communists, with date

of progress, the U.S. eventually moved the bombing farther and farther north, without any significant tactical results. The North Vietnamese moved no closer to negotiations; as the bombing intensified, so did the Vietnamese resistance.

In late January 1968, the Vietcong caught the U.S. offguard in the Tet Offensive. During the celebrations of the lunar new year, the Vietcong struck simultaneously at the U.S. embassy and several cities, towns, and villages throughout South Vietnam. Though the United States quickly responded, ultimately winning the battles, the offensive marked a turning point in the war. Tet demonstrated that the United States could not easily win the war and that the Vietcong could endure for some time. Furthermore, the psychological impact was profound. Tet changed the opinion of thousands in the United States. Within two months of its initiation, Johnson announced he would not seek re-election.

The end of the war saw the return of 591 American prisoners-of-war, though some 2,413 remain unaccounted for.

On an increasing tide of anti-war demonstrations and the departure of draft evaders to exile in Canada, Richard Nixon won the 1968 elections as the candidate to end the war in Vietnam. His plans, however, were contradictory. He intended to withdraw U.S. troops in the policy of "Vietnamization," which trained South Vietnamese forces to assume major combat roles, without any explanation of how he expected the South Vietnamese to win without the Americans, who had not prevailed against the Vietcong themselves. Nixon also ordered increased bombing of the North, even though previous bombing had proved strategically ineffective. The North did not move closer to concessions in the subsequent negotiations. Nixon illegally widened the war to include massive bombing raids on Cambodia and Laos, followed by ground incursions against the Ho Chi Minh Trail. The North waited for the U.S. to leave.

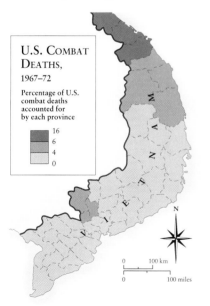

U.S. COMBAT DEATHS,
1967–72

Percentage of U.S. combat deaths accounted for by each province

16
6
4
0

0   100 km

0   100 miles

Without progress in the negotiations, Nixon ordered an intensive bombing of the North, known as the Christmas bombings, afterwards listed by Swedish Prime Minister Olaf Palme as among the worst atrocities of the twentieth century. By January 1973, the negotiations were concluded, and within weeks the majority of the U.S. troops had left Vietnam. The North Vietnamese ultimately captured Saigon in May 1975, renaming it Ho Chi Minh City.

U.S. casualties numbered over 58,000, while Vietnamese casualties were estimated to be two million.

UNITED STATES AND LATIN AMERICA SINCE 1945

While the Soviet Union was extending its control over the states of Eastern Europe, the United States had already established an order in the Western Hemisphere amenable to its interests. The difference between the "hard" empire the Soviets exercised in Eastern Europe and the "soft" empire the United States operated in Central and parts of South America are matters for continued historical debate. Since 1945, the United States has been engaged in maintaining the system and punishing regional deviants.

Under Article 51 of the UN Charter, the United States could seek a special dispensation to deal with regional bodies. It was of course an indispensable article to ensure the survival of the Monroe Doctrine. The 1905 amendment gave the United States "police powers" and therefore U.S. preeminence in the Western Hemisphere. Washington moved quickly to encourage most of the nations to suppress the local Communist parties. Despite widespread compliance, the major threat did not come from the normally conservative Communist parties, but usually from the more radical revolutionary movements or reform governments.

The social reform government initiated by Guatemalan leader Aravelo in 1944 and continued by Arbenz in 1950 was the first significant victim of CIA operations in the postwar period. After the introduction of a series of reforms in the labor laws, agriculture, land, and suffrage, and the expropriation of United Fruit Company land, the CIA facilitated the removal of the Arbenz government in 1954. Despite little connection with the Soviet Union, Washington portrayed the situation as a threat to the United States and the Western Hemisphere.

The largest thorn in Washington's side was Cuba, perhaps because the revolution took place against a government closely connected to the United States. After years of activity, in January 1959, a movement led by Fidel Castro overthrew the Batista government. The Kennedy administration launched an abortive invasion of the island by Cuban exiles in April 1961. The invasion was a fiasco, and remained an enduring failure for the Kennedy administration. Following the invasion, Cuba negotiated various arms agreements with the Soviet Union. By the summer of 1962, Moscow had shipped missiles to Cuba that were operative by October. When U.S. intelligence discoverd the missile sites, a thirteen-day crisis ensued. In the end, Moscow agreed to remove the missiles in return for a U.S. pledge not to invade Cuba and the subsequent U.S. removal of its Jupiter missiles from Turkey.

Each subsequent U.S. administration engaged in either overt or covert force against various governments or movements in Latin America. President Johnson intervened in Brazil in 1964 and in the Dominican Republic in 1965. President Nixon's actions and decisions contributed to the deposing of the Allende government in Chile in 1973; the Reagan administration exacerbated the region-wide crisis in Central America during the 1980s, particularly in its attempt to depose the Sandinista government in Nicaragua. The United States invaded Panama in December 1989; and vetoed UN Security Council resolutions condemning the action.

In a more humanitarian gesture, the Clinton administration sent U.S. troops into Haiti to protect its citizens in 1994. Cuba continues to remain isolated by the United States as of 1998.

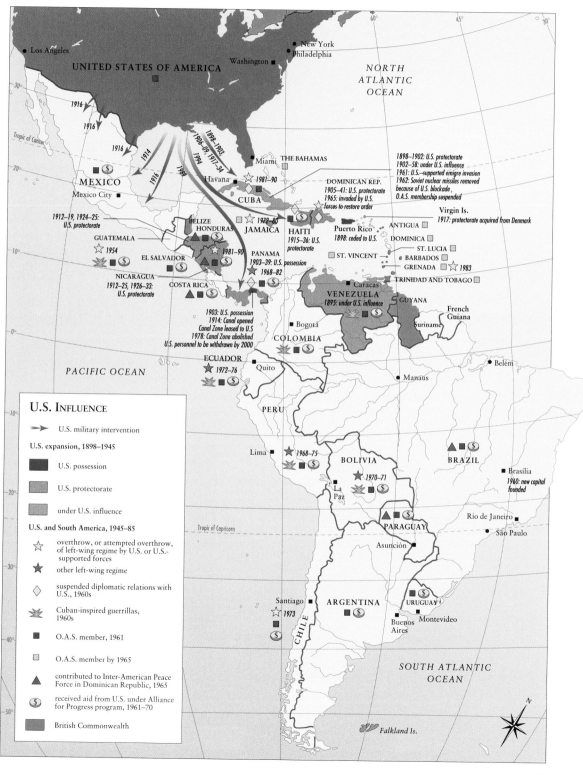

Los Angeles

UNITED STATES OF AMERICA

NORTH
ATLANTIC
OCEAN

New York
Washington Philadelphia

Tropic of Cancer

1916

1916

1916

1914

1916

1898–1903

1906–09, 1917–34

1994

Miami

THE BAHAMAS

MEXICO

Mexico City

Havana

1981–90

CUBA

1898–1902: U.S. protectorate
1902–58: under U.S. influence
1961: U.S.–supported emigre invasion
1962: Soviet nuclear missiles removed
because of U.S. blockade,
O.A.S. membership suspended

DOMINICAN REP.
1905–41: U.S. protectorate
1965: invaded by U.S.
forces to restore order

Virgin Is.
1917: protectorate acquired from Denmark

1912–19, 1924–25:
U.S. protectorate

BELIZE

HONDURAS

JAMAICA

1972–80

HAITI
1915–36: U.S.
protectorate

Puerto Rico
1898: ceded to U.S.

ANTIGUA

DOMINICA

GUATEMALA
1954

1981–90

ST. LUCIA

ST. VINCENT

BARBADOS

GRENADA 1983

EL SALVADOR

PANAMA
1903–39: U.S. possession

1968–82

TRINIDAD AND TOBAGO

NICARAGUA
1912–25, 1926–33:
U.S. protectorate

COSTA RICA

Caracas

VENEZUELA
1895: under U.S. influence

GUYANA

French
Guiana

1903: U.S. possession
1914: Canal opened
Canal Zone leased to U.S
1978: Canal Zone abolished
U.S. personnel to be withdrawn by 2000

Bogotá

Suriname

COLOMBIA

PACIFIC OCEAN

ECUADOR
1972–76

Quito

Belém

Manaus

PERU

Lima

1968–75

BOLIVIA

1970–71

BRAZIL

Brasília
1960: new capital
founded

La
Paz

Tropic of Capricorn

PARAGUAY

Asunción

Río de Janeiro

São Paulo

U.S. INFLUENCE

U.S. military intervention

U.S. expansion, 1898–1945

U.S. possession

U.S. protectorate

under U.S. influence

U.S. and South America, 1945–85

overthrow, or attempted overthrow,
of left-wing regime by U.S. or U.S.-
supported forces

other left-wing regime

suspended diplomatic relations with
U.S., 1960s

Cuban-inspired guerrillas,
1960s

O.A.S. member, 1961

O.A.S. member by 1965

contributed to Inter-American Peace
Force in Dominican Republic, 1965

received aid from U.S. under Alliance
for Progress program, 1961–70

British Commonwealth

Santiago

1973

ARGENTINA

URUGUAY

Montevideo

Buenos
Aires

CHILE

SOUTH ATLANTIC
OCEAN

N

Falkland Is.

135

CIVIL RIGHTS

"I've been to the mountain top. I've looked over, and I've seen the promised land. I may not get there with you, but I want you to know tonight that we as a people will get to the promised land. So, I'm happy tonight." *Martin Luther King, Jr.*, speech at Memphis, April 3, 1968—the day before his assassination

The legacy of slavery and Reconstruction in the United States was systemic racial discrimination that restricted the access of African Americans to the best-quality education, limited their voting rights, and caused stark disadvantages in jobs and housing. The Civil Rights movement that gathered force in the 1950s pressed for change on all fronts. Triggered by two events—the 1954 Supreme Court decision *Brown v. Board of Education*, which unanimously declared "separate but equal" education unconstitutional, and in December 1955 the refusal by Rosa Parks, a black seamstress on her way home by bus, to give up her seat to a white passenger—and fueled by the leadership of Reverend Dr. Martin Luther King, Jr., the movement started in the South and quickly swept nationwide. Through the 1950s and 1960s sympathizers mobilized large public demonstrations in support of an end to racial discrimination.

The movement succeeded in altering the national perspective on civil rights. In 1964 Congress passed, and President Lyndon Johnson signed, a Civil Rights Act protecting voting rights, employment rights, and rights of access to "places of public accommodation." Yet serious disparities persisted. Demonstrations in Selma, Alabama, over voting rights in 1965, and marches in Washington, D.C., and many other places kept the issue of civil rights in the public eye. Attempts to integrate schools by busing black children to white districts often met with violent opposition from white communities. Little investment was made in economically depressed black communities, where housing and education continued to deteriorate. President Johnson's "War on Poverty" was an attempt to allocate government funding to fight hunger, poverty, and discrimination, but on the election of republican Richard Nixon to the presidency in 1968 these programs began to be phased out. For many, the disparity between promises and actual results led to a keen sense of disappointment that burst into urban riots, especially after Rev. King was assassinated in 1968.

By the late 1990s African Americans were still disadvantaged on average in terms of affluence, education, housing, income, and other social indicators. Racial isolation still existed in housing and education, and urban decay was accelerated by drugs, violence, and hopelessness. In the general population and among legislators, a growing distaste for the processes of "affirmation action," which offered extra help designed to redress past discrimination against blacks, threatened to slow down the recent progress. However, the number of African-American elected officials had risen from just over one thousand in 1970 to 11,500 in the 1990s; a clearly identifiable black middle class had arisen; and the contributions of African Americans had reached every part of American society.

"Movement politics" has become a shorthand for a collection of strategies and tactics used by African Americans and adopted by others in pursuit of their human rights. The "women's movement" coalesced in the 1960s around issues of equal pay and sex discrimination. Public demonstrations maintained a high profile for these issues while court cases, lobbying, and election campaigns put them on the political agenda. In the 1970s the political effort concentrated on an attempt to get an Equal Rights Amendment addressing sex equality added to the U.S. Constitution. The amendment fell short of ratification by fifteen states, mostly in the southeast and the southwest, but the national debate prompted several states to pass their own equality legislation and increased awareness of women's political and economic issues. By the late 1990s women had made appreciable strides in achieving prominent positions in business, government, law, and medicine. Even so, women still earned about 25 percent less than men, and senior positions in business and government were still predominantly occupied by men.

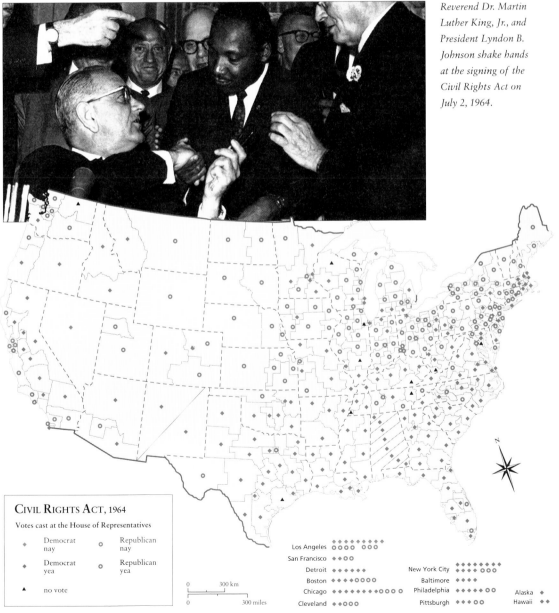

Reverend Dr. Martin Luther King, Jr., and President Lyndon B. Johnson shake hands at the signing of the Civil Rights Act on July 2, 1964.

CIVIL RIGHTS ACT, 1964

Votes cast at the House of Representatives

- ◆ Democrat nay
- ○ Republican nay
- ◆ Democrat yea
- ○ Republican yea
- ▲ no vote

0 ___ 300 km
0 ___ 300 miles

Los Angeles ◆◆◆◆◆◆◆◆◆◆ ○○○○ ○○○
San Francisco ◆◆○○
Detroit ◆◆◆◆◆◆
Boston ◆◆◆◆○○○○
Chicago ◆◆◆◆◆◆◆◆○○○○ ○
Cleveland ◆◆○○○

New York City ◆◆◆◆◆◆◆◆◆ ○○○○
Baltimore ◆◆◆◆
Philadelphia ◆◆◆◆◆○○
Pittsburgh ◆◆◆○○

Alaska ◆
Hawaii ◆◆

INTERNAL MIGRATION SINCE 1945

After World War II, many city dwellers wanted their own place in the sun. William Levitt led a suburban expansion, building thousands of affordable homes. In the late 1940s, a veteran could move in with no deposit, paying just 56 dollars per month.

The United States and Canada have highly mobile populations, but the rate of movement has changed slightly over time. In the immediate post–Second World War period, population movement increased, and by the early 1960s over 20 percent of the population was moving residence annually. This rate settled down in the 1980s and 1990s to about 16 percent moving each year. Most of this movement is localized: about two out of three movers do not leave the county of their former residence, and only one out of six relocate to a different state or province.

Even relatively localized movement can have significant impact, however. The most obvious result of the last half-century of migration has been the suburbanization of cities. Suburbs, with a little more space and situated a little less close to old industrial centers, have always been attractive residential areas. Their availability depends on the accessibility of transportation and the cost of housing. In the wake of the Second World War, developments in the house-building industry brought down the cost of houses; suburban tracts of land provided the ideal place for mass production of detached homes and government subsidized highways; increased ownership of cars allowed efficient access to these plots; and government-underwritten mortgage and veterans' benefits schemes made available the credit needed to purchase. The growth of the American middle class, booming business, and government encouragement combined to stimulate massive suburban growth.

While suburban living costs had declined, there were still people who could not afford to move, or who found their path blocked by racial discrimination. Inner cities became increasingly disadvantaged as industry and retailing also moved to the open spaces of the suburbs. City centers have maintained a role as locations of business administration and cultural institutions; they continue to house a proportion of affluent persons for whom urban contact is important; they have become more attractive as the decline and relocation of heavy industry has led to an improved environment. Nevertheless, by 1990, over half of America's population lived in suburbs, and most of these now find their employment, shopping, and entertainment in the suburbs.

The second half of the twentieth century has also seen a regional shift in the population toward the south and west in the United States. The U.S. Bureau of the Census calculates the geographical position of the "mean center of population" after each census. In 1940, this center was inside the borders of Indiana; by 1990, it had moved significantly south and west, to Crawford County, Missouri. A similar but less pronounced shift occurred in Canada. In Mexico rural people moved to the cities, particularly Mexico City, and many more Mexicans worked just over the U.S. border, returning home each day. Migrant Mexican workers took jobs on U.S. farms, in government service, and in the construction industries.

These areas have become increasingly accessible to creative investment, with the development of an efficient transport system, a highly developed trucking industry, and domestic air service. The "sunbelt," a crescent of sunny states reaching from North Carolina in the east through Texas to California in the west, has a climate with evident attractions, and its excesses have been made bearable by a vast increase in the use of air-conditioning in homes, offices, and factories. Relatively inexpensive land and labor costs, state government incentives, and a non-unionized workforce all promoted investment and development. The decline of heavy industry and the parallel growth of light engineering and service industry have also allowed areas of development to be less tied to the location of raw materials. For information-based modern industries, such as software development, the raw material is an educated population, and in this field the universities of the West rival those of the Northeast in excellence.

Throughout the post–Second World War period, the Northeast and Midwest have shown weaker employment profiles than the South and West. Recessions have hit harder, and recovery has come more slowly in the Northeast and Midwest than in the South and West. This regional pattern looks likely to continue into the beginning of the twenty-first century.

NET REGIONAL
MIGRATION, 1940–60

— limit of population zone

➡ black migration

➡ white migration

2,000 approximate
1,000 number
0 of migrants in thousands

•—• cross-border twin cities

IMMIGRATION SINCE 1950

Immigration during the latter part of the 20th century has dramatically added to the human diversity visible in most North American cities.

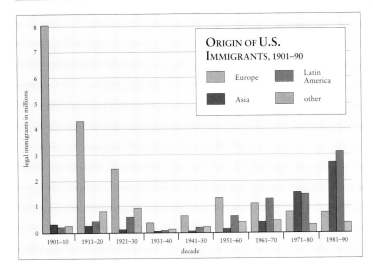

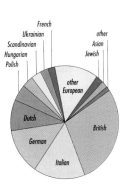

French
Ukrainian
Scandinavian
Hungarian
Polish

other
Asian
Jewish

other European

Dutch

British

German

Italian

ORIGIN OF IMMIGRANTS IN CANADA, c. 1961

The proportion of foreign-born in the U.S. and Canadian populations reached its twentieth-century peak around 1910, and many immigrants into Canada later moved south into the U.S. In the 1920s the U.S. tightened immigration restrictions, reducing the inflow for some decades. In 1965, the immigration regulations were altered to favor applicants with useful skills and those with close family relations already in the United States. In addition, the United States accepts many refugees annually; others manage to enter the country without permission. In 1986, 2.6 million of these were granted amnesty, but illegal immigrants continue to arrive and are estimated to account for about one-fifth of the United States' foreign-born population.

Toward the end of the twentieth century, there was a boom in immigration. In 1996, the United States admitted 916,000 immigrants, and there were significant numbers of illegal entries. The total number of foreign-born permanent residents reached around twenty million persons. While this accounts for less than 10 percent of the total population, the current rate of movement is expected to continue.

ORIGIN OF U.S. IMMIGRANTS, 1901–90

Europe
Latin America
Asia
other

legal immigrants in millions

8
7
6
5
4
3
2
1
0

1901–10 1911–20 1921–30 1931–40 1941–50 1951–60 1961–70 1971–80 1981–90

decade

There has been a shift in the national origins of immigrants. In the 1950s, over half of immigrants to the United States came from Europe. In the 1960s, this showed a sharp drop to about one-third of all immigration, and fell again to less than 18 percent in the 1970s. The main growth has been in immigration from Asia and Latin America. A move to the United States has long been the goal of many economically pressed or politically oppressed people around the world. Changes in conditions in other countries can therefore have a distinct effect on the pattern of immigration to the United States. The disruption of war in Southeast Asia stimulated population movements in the 1970s and 1980s; political and economic pressures in Central America have led to a demand for entry to the United States from a variety of countries; and the collapse of author-itarian governments in the former Soviet Union and its satel-lites has released new populations into the immigration flow.

American employers engaged in low-wage industries are not slow to exploit the availability of this labor pool. For the most part, however, these immigrants have entered the United States motivated to do as well as they can, and their ambitions may be fulfilled in succeeding generations, rather than immediately.

Recent immigration has affected some states particularly. Over three-quar-ters of immigrants in the 1980s settled in the six states of California, New York, Florida, Texas, Illinois, and New Jersey, with California receiving a dispropor-tionate 38 percent of the national total. As well as offering jobs and similar advantages, these states have proximity to immigrant entry points: California and Texas share borders with Mexico, Florida faces the Caribbean, and major entry airports are located in Chicago, New York, and New Jersey.

Young people and families are heavily represented in immigrant populations; therefore, waves of immigration have an echo effect for at least a generation. The family-preference regulations of American law provide another multiplier for any immigrant group. As immigrant groups settle and have families, the long-term ethnic shape of the nation is affected. It is projected that by halfway through the twenty-first century, about 25 percent of the U.S. population will be from Hispanic roots, 14 percent black, and 8 percent Asian, although marriage patterns may make such distinctions less relevant.

RESIDENTS OF
HISPANIC ORIGINS,
1990

1,000,000 and over
500,000 to 999,999
100,000 to 499,999
under 100,000

Components of the top 8
Hispanic populations,
by U.S. states

Mexican

Puerto Rican

Cuban

other

Components of Hispanic
populations,
by Canadian provinces

Salvadoran

Mexican

Guatemalan

CANADA: REGIONAL POLITICS

For over a hundred years, the Canadian party political system featured two major parties. Smaller parties played a part, but a duopoly dominated. The Liberals and the Progressive Conservatives have continued to form governments up to the end of the twentieth century, but this consistency disguises a varied political geography. The linguistic and cultural differences between the Anglophone and Francophone populations are long-standing. With the addition of later immigration, Canada has become a multicultural community.

The population is concentrated into a small part of the nation's huge area, with over a quarter of the nation's population in Québec, and greater than one-third in Ontario. The Maritime provinces are home to less than one-tenth of the population, while the three prairie provinces, with the Pacific coast province of British Columbia, account for more than a quarter. Canadians are concentrated in the southern parts of these provinces.

The variations in economics, cultures, and settlement patterns provide the foundations for political differences. Provincial and territorial governments have significant policy and spending powers. They also provide

borders within which these differences across the nation can develop political voices through regionally relevant political parties.

As recently as the election of 1984, the Progressive Conservatives, taking the vast majority of seats, could claim nationwide support. The Liberals, with forty seats concentrated in Ontario, Québec, and the Maritimes, and the New Democrats' thirty seats in Ontario and the West, showed some regional bias. The Conservative government pressed free trade reform, debating the cultural and economic power of the United States and raising fears of decline in previously protected Canadian industries. Reelected in 1988, the Conservative majority fell dramaticaly, while the Liberals and the New Democrats continued to show their different regional strengths.

Tackling the long-standing problem of the position of Québec in Canada, the Conservatives led the way to the Meech Lake Accord, recognizing Québec as a "distinct society" within Canada. When Manitoba failed to support the plan, and Newfoundland withdrew its support, the Accord was abandoned in 1990. There followed the Charlottetown Agreement, an attempt to respond to criticisms of earlier proposals, but this was defeated when just over half of those voting in a 1992 national referendum voted against it.

The Meech Lake and Charlottetown debates had provided a firm regional context in which other divisions, for example, over economic policy, were aired. Québec separatists saw little more to be gained from their traditional allegiance at the federal level with the Progressive Conservatives. Westerners similarly failed to believe that the mainstream political parties were any longer representing their interests. The Bloc Québecois and the Reform Party emerged to fill the vacuum, and at the 1993 election the Progressive Conservative Party almost disappeared, winning only two seats (of 295). The Bloc Québecois' seats were all in Québec; about 90 percent of the Reform Party's seats were in British Columbia and Alberta; the reduced New Democrats remained a western party; only the Liberals had seats in all parts of the country.

Before the next federal election, Québec held a provincial referendum on sovereignty that was very narrowly defeated, yet kept the issue of regionalism prominent. The 1997 election saw the Liberals retain-

CANADA ETHNIC VOTE

Origins of predominant groupings

- British Isles (English, Welsh, Scottish, or Irish)
- French
- Scandinavian
- Central and East Europeans

ing government with a reduced majority. While well ahead of its rivals, the redistribution of seats emphasized the regionalism of Canadian politics. The Reform Party's seats are all in the West, and while the New Democrats made gains in the Maritimes, they remain a party of the geographic periphery. The Bloc Québecois, with a falling number of seats, remains a one-province party, and the Progressive Conservatives have become oriented to the east of the country. Over three-quarters of the Liberal Party's seats were won in Ontario and Québec. This party too began to look like a regional entity. Canada faced the beginning of the twenty-first century with a new system of regional political parties at the national level.

U.S. ELECTORAL POLITICS SINCE THE 1960s

STATES CARRIED BY REPUBLICANS IN PRESIDENTIAL ELECTIONS, 1968–88

- held in every election
- held in 5 out of 6 elections
- held in 4 out of 6 elections
- held in 3 out of 6 elections
- held in 2 out of 6 elections
- held only once

> "If a free society cannot help the many who are poor, it cannot save the few who are rich."
>
> *John F. Kennedy*, Inaugural Address, January 1961

The domination of the South and West in population growth has significant political implications. Each decennial census is followed by a redistribution of political representation to reflect intervening changes in the distribution of population. On each occasion, the 435 seats in the U.S. House of Representatives are reallocated between states according to relative population size. This also has an impact on each state's strength in the presidential electoral college, which rises or declines in parallel with its number of members of Congress.

In the last presidential election of the 1950s, the Northeast held 133 of the nation's electoral college votes (then totaling 531), and the Midwest had a further 153. The South at that time controlled 166 electoral college votes, and the West had seventy-nine. In Congress the balance was 115 House seats in the Northeast, 129 in the Midwest, 134 in the South, fifty-seven in the West. By the 1990s, population and political authority shifted south and west, as their number of electoral college votes increased to 184 and 119 respectively (from a current total of 538), while the Northeast and Midwest saw their number drop to 106 and 129. The shift of power was mirrored in Congress, which in the 1990s had only eighty-eight House members from the Northeast and 105 from the Midwest, while there were 149 from the South, and ninety-three from the West. Census projections for 2000 and 2010 suggest that at the turn of the century a further transfer will take place of around eleven congressional seats and electoral college votes from the Northeast and Midwest to the South and West, with about nine more following suit a decade later. From a position where the Northeast and Midwest controlled over half of the presidential electoral vote, its share will fall below 40 percent of the national total.

The shift has implications for any national policies with regional impact, as elected officials go to the federal capital in Washington to compete for the interests of their regions. Also, the shift of power moved toward regions that voted relatively conservatively in recent decades. It was expected that results would show a benefit for Republican Party candidates, but by the 1990s, the political trends were not uniform nationwide. The mountain states shifted more firmly toward conservative politics, but in the Pacific Northwest moderate political patterns were reinforced, and California emerged as a highly competitive state on the national scene.

In the South there was a considerable realignment of political support away from being a "solid Democratic" region toward being the part of the nation to show by far the most support for the Republican Party at the congressional as well as the presidential level. In the person of Newt Gingrich, Georgia provided the first Southern Republican Speaker of the U.S. House of Representatives in 1993, and the addition of Mississippian Trent Lott as Majority Leader of the U.S. Senate added more Republican political leadership from the South. The rise of this region had also moderated the politics of the Democratic Party, and while the Southern credentials of Bill Clinton (Arkansas) and Al Gore (Tennessee) may not have won over the southern white vote to the Democratic Party, they did provide the basis of a coalition between liberal and moderate voters to give an overall national victory for their party in the 1996 presidential election.

Traditionally in U.S. history a dominant political party has been able to gain victory at presidential and congressional levels, acting to unite the branches of government under a party's leadership. Of the fifteen elections between 1968 and 1996, only three gave one party control over the presidency, Senate, and House, as the electorate has chosen to separate national power between the major political parties with a consistency that has made the late twentieth century a unique period in American political history.

VOTE FOR PRESIDENT IN THE SOUTH, 1968–88

- Republican majority in at least 5 out of 6 elections
- Republican majority in 4 elections
- Republicans and Democrats each carried state 3 times
- Democrat majority in 4 elections
- Democrat majority in at least 5 elections

N

| 0 | | 200 km |

| 0 | | 200 miles |

REAGAN DOCTRINE/END OF THE COLD WAR

During the period of détente (1969–1979) between the United States and the Soviet Union, the U.S. refused to intervene significantly in regional conflicts under President Carter. In this atmosphere, fourteen revolutions were conducted in the Third World. Ronald Reagan came to the presidency promising to reinvigorate U.S. power and prestige, to conduct a more assertive foreign policy, and ultimately to confine Soviet power to the "ash heap of history."

Specifically, the Reagan Doctrine was an attempt to "roll back" what were presented as Soviet gains in the Third World, especially in Nicaragua, Angola, Afghanistan, and Cambodia. To bring this about, the United States initiated a series of "low-intensity conflicts," supporting in each region indigenous forces who operated out of neighboring countries against the variety of leftist forces that held power in the four named countries. Only in Afghanistan was the United States assisting the *mujahadeen* to conduct warfare against the direct intervention of Soviet troops. In Nicaragua, Washington fought the Sandinista revolution, resulting in thousands of Nicaraguan deaths, even though their connections with the Soviet Union were minimal, their revolution was by no means Soviet directed, and they could hardly be said to provide Moscow with an outpost in the Caribbean. Nevertheless, the United States could be seen as persistent in these regional conflicts, its perceived power and thereby its prestige being greatly enhanced.

Concurrently, the Reagan administration continued and heightened the bipolar hostility with the Soviet Union following its invasion of Afghanistan. The first term of the Reagan administration (1981–1985) is often referred to as the period of the second Cold War. During this period, Reagan further increased the U.S. expenditure on defense and initiated the "Star Wars" program, officially known as the Strategic Defense Initiative (SDI). The technical idea was to provide a protective shield against Soviet nuclear attack (it was discontinued in 1993). The goal was to increase the pressure on the Soviet Union to the point where it would not be able to compete with the United States.

The tense atmosphere of the early Reagan years was transformed by the relentless initiatives of Mikhail Gorbachev, who came to power in the Soviet Union in March 1985. From that year onward, a series of Superpower summits were held every year until the end of the Cold War. The Soviet leader initiated a series of reforms to slow the decline of the Soviet Union through *glasnost* (liberalization), *perestroika* (economic development), and "New Thinking." Despite these efforts to save the Soviet Union, its power began to visibly wane in the Third World from 1988 on, when decisions were made to suspend aid to Third World regimes and pull out from the most acute problem of Afghanistan.

More symbolic and more dramatic were the events of 1989. Following the opening of the border between Hungary and Austria, thousands moved west. Hundreds of thousands gathered in the city squares across Eastern Europe, which brought about the collapse of the Warsaw Pact and the Communist system that had been imposed on the region since the 1940s. The Berlin Wall was torn down in November 1989, and the Cold War was largely declared over.

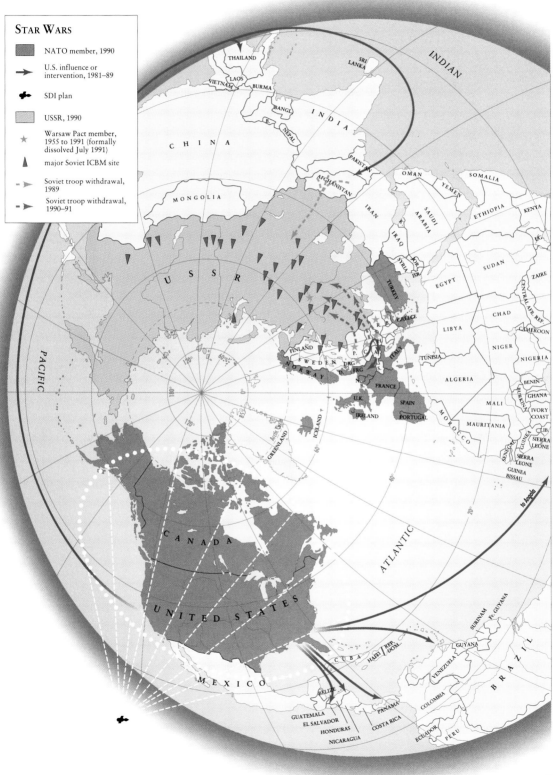

STAR WARS

NATO member, 1990

U.S. influence or
intervention, 1981–89

SDI plan

USSR, 1990

Warsaw Pact member,
1955 to 1991 (formally
dissolved July 1991)

major Soviet ICBM site

Soviet troop withdrawal,
1989

Soviet troop withdrawal,
1990–91

THE NEW WORLD ORDER

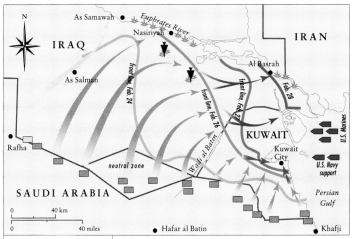

DESERT STORM,
FEB. 24–MARCH 2,
1991

☐ French army unit

▨ U.S. army unit

▨ British army unit

▨ Arab army unit

🏹 Allied advance

☘ Allied bombing

▼ airbase

The phrase the "New World Order" was commonly in use during the early 1990s, following the collapse of Soviet power in Eastern Europe, the end of the Cold War, and ultimately the disintegration of the Soviet Union in 1991. The phrase referred more to the mood of the period and the aspirations for a new direction after the protracted period of the Cold War than to any particular new configuration of power. Despite the public euphoria at the end of the Cold War, the major powers were disconcerted at the lack of direction and diminished cohesion among the Western alliance in the absence of a clearly identifiable "enemy."

As the Cold War was being declared over, the United States conducted a swift and decisive invasion of Panama to remove Manuel Noriega from power. In many ways the action was reminiscent of U.S. interventions that occurred both during the Cold War and in the early decades of the twentieth century.

The most significant conflict associated with the "New World Order" was the Persian Gulf war of 1991. While this "second Gulf war," between the UN coalition and Iraq, originated in the politics of oil and previous regional tensions, the immediate crisis resulted from the Iraqi invasion of Kuwait in August 1990. The Security Council passed a series of twelve resolutions between August 2 and November 29, 1990, including the authorization to use "all necessary means" to expel Iraq from Kuwait. Close to half a million U.S. troops were dispatched to the area to operate what was referred to as Desert Shield.

A formidable array of forces was gathered under coalition forces from a variety of thirty-eight countries, including several Middle Eastern countries, to form one of the largest fighting forces in history. Despite considerable potential for the forced withdrawal of Iraq from Kuwait through the use of continued sanctions and/or negotiations, the stated conditions could not be met by the imposed deadline of January 15, 1991. The Gulf war was largely a six-week-long use of disproportionate air power against Iraqi forces that put up little resistance; the air force partially deserted to Iran, and 175,000 Iraqi troops surrendered with limited resistance. An estimated 200,000 people were killed in the conflict.

After forty-three days of air power conflict, the ground war lasted a matter of days before Iraq surrendered and agreed to withdraw and comply with the UN directives. Despite the resounding victory for the U.S.-led coalition forces and the pulverization of parts of Iraqi society, Saddam Hussein remained in power, which curtailed the U.S. euphoria.

As the Bush administration concentrated on the political aspects of the New World Order, economic rivals in Europe (with a unified Germany at the center) began and in Asia (with Japan at the center) a challenge to U.S. supremacy in the economic realm.

The extension of power, exemplified by this U.S. fleet of aircraft carriers. These huge warships can sail within striking distance to almost any point on earth.

THE NEW WORLD ORDER

- United States and allies, c. 1991
- Russia and other CIS states
- potential for NATO new members

U.S. active-duty military personnel, September 1994

10,000 — number in countries having more than 500 personnel
0 —

FREE TRADE

The North American Free Trade Agreement (NAFTA), signed by Canada, Mexico, and the United States, came into force on January 1, 1994. At its formation, it was the world's largest trade bloc in terms of the combined gross national product of the three member nations. It also had the unusual feature of being a trading entity composed of two highly developed countries, the United States and Canada, and a developing nation, Mexico, with Third World wage scales and great social problems.

In the decades before 1990, any idea of a commercial union between Mexico and the United States was highly unlikely; furthermore, it would have been ruled out of hand in Mexico among influential circles and the intelligentsia. Nonetheless, the pattern since the 1940s of ever closer trade and investment relations between the two countries was crystal clear. Mexico's efforts to chart an independent path to national development broke down in the 1980s, when the nation's foreign debt crisis of 1982 dragged it into the mire of a deep recession. This in turn threatened to destabilize the position of the country's ruling party, the Institutional Revolutionary Party, which had monopolized political power in the land since the 1920s. Consequently, Mexican president Carlos Salinas de Gortari (1988–1994) proved highly receptive to the overtures of President George Bush for the creation of a free trade area by the two nations. Treaty negotiations began in 1990; by February 1991, the deliberations included Canada, which had already concluded a free trade agreement with the United States in 1988. By 1992, the tripartite discussions were finished and the NAFTA treaty was signed. A year later, Canadian Prime Minister Mulroney, President Clinton, and President Salinas were successful in obtaining the ratification of the trade agreement.

NAFTA immediately removed many of the trade and investment barriers standing in the way of increased commerce; it also set a maximum deadline of fifteen years for the complete removal of all such restrictions. Restrictions in certain activities, such as the automotive and financial sectors in Mexico, were to be phased out over a ten- to fifteen-year period. Certain critical areas were to be excluded from any investment liberalization such as petroleum in Mexico, the cultural domain in Canada, and airline and radio communications in the United States.

The emergence of NAFTA was of major significance to the three nations, above all to the United States and Mexico. It continued and accelerated the upward trend of U.S.–Mexican bilateral trade, which rose from 28 billion dollars in 1980 to 130 billion dollars by 1997. Mexico was thus able to supplant Japan as the second largest export market for the United States, Canada retaining first place. Of course, Mexico's position as one of the prime markets for American goods has not been due to NAFTA alone, but also to the economic reforms of Mexico in the 1980s and 1990s, which created a more open and less protected domestic market.

Politically, NAFTA has not had a great impact upon internal politics in Mexico and Canada, but in the United States the repercussions have been enor-

NORTH AMERICA'S
SLICE OF WORLD
GDP, 1994

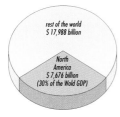

rest of the world
$ 17,988 billion

North
America
$ 7,676 billion
(30% of the Wold GDP)

mous. There, trade unionists, environmentalists, and many Democratic Party politicians have been die-hard opponents of the treaty on the ground that it would cause a migration of jobs and investment to low-wage Mexico. President Clinton and his pro-NAFTA allies were successful, however, in countering the case against ratification by arguing that the free trade area would open up new export opportunities and hence create employment for American workers. Both the pro- and anti-treaty camps seriously overstated the actual impact that NAFTA would have on the vast U.S. economy. Massive job losses did not occur, but neither was there any appreciable NAFTA-produced job creation. Mexico's financial crisis of 1995, which provoked a sharp recession in that country, limited U.S. export growth to that destination and meant that new job creation did not offset the relatively modest employment losses that NAFTA caused in vulnerable industries. What did occur, however, was that NAFTA became an extremely contentious issue in American politics. Since 1995, it has generated some of the fiercest trade battles to be seen between the White House and Congress since the 1930s. This has meant that Congress has been unwilling to grant the president a free hand in negotiating new free trade agreements with nations in Latin America.

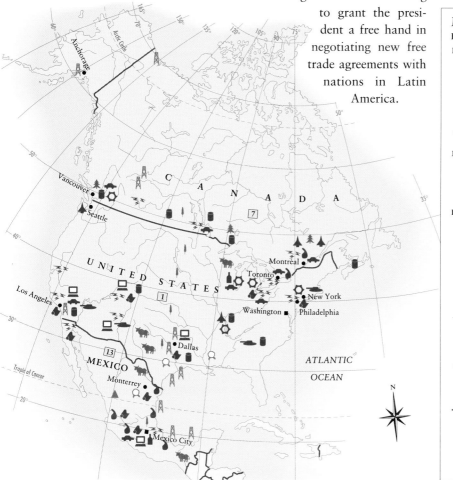

MAJOR ACTIVITIES IN NORTH AMERICA

Forestry and agriculture

- timber
- wheat
- cotton
- cattle

Mining

- oil and gas
- silver

Industry

- brewing
- food processing
- textile
- chemicals
- electronics
- engineering
- vehicles
- aerospace
- defense industry
- computers
- [1] Gross National Product World ranking, 1997

151

CHRONOLOGY

13,000 BC Cave-dwelling.

10,000 BC Hunting and fishing.

7000 BC Migrants from Asia in northwest; semi-permanent settlements.

4500 BC Mound-building along the Mississippi River.

3000 BC Aleut and Inuit migrants from Siberia; use of copper. Permanent settlements in Great Lakes area. Permanent settlements in Tehuacán (Mexico). Spread of agriculture.

2500 BC Growth of towns and cities in Central America. Emergence of religion. Manufacture of textiles, ceramics. Settlements in Georgia and Florida.

1200 BC Emergence of Olmec civilization in Mexico.

1000 BC Development of Adena culture in the northeast; mound-building spreads.

300 BC The earliest Maya cities established (Central America). Adena culture declines in northeast; emergence of Hopewell Indian chiefdoms.

AD 50 Growth of Teotihuacán (Mexico).

AD 300 Mayan civilization flourishing throughout Central America.

AD 500 Hopewell Indians in decline.

AD 700 Hohokam and Anasazi cultures in Southwest. Use of bow and arrow spreads.

AD 900 Mayan civilization superseded by Toltec in Central America.

AD 950 Chaco "pueblos" in the Southwest.

AD 986 Viking settlements in Greenland.

AD 1000 Mogollon culture in Southwest; stone houses. Viking settlements in Vinland (Nova Scotia).

1050 Major settlements along Mississippi. Inuit spread into Greenland.

1100 Anasazi culture in Arizona, New Mexico, Utah, and Colorado.

1200 Anasazi oust Hohokam in Southwest. Mound-building in Alabama.

1492 Columbus reaches the West Indies.

1493 First Spanish settlement in Hispaniola (Haiti/Dominica).

1497 English John Cabot reaches Newfoundland.

1513 Spanish Ponce de Léon claims Florida.

1520 Magellan crosses the Pacific Ocean.

1524 Italian Verrazano begins explorations of North American coast.

1539 Spanish Coronado and de Soto start exploration of Florida and Great Plains.

1545 Discovery of silver at Zacatecas in Mexico.

1550 Europeans introduce horses and guns. French trading in Canada.

1585 English settlement at Roanoke Island.

1598 Spanish settlers from Mexico reach Rio Grande.

1607 English settlement at Jamestown, Virginia.

1608 French settlements in Québec.

1610 Spanish settlement at Santa Fe (New Mexico).

1620 From England the *Mayflower* (Pilgrim Fathers) reaches Plymouth.

1625 Dutch establish New Amsterdam.

1630 English Puritans start settling Massachusetts.

1636 Foundation of Harvard, first university. Pequot war between English settlers and Indians. Swedish settlement on Delaware River.

1639 English establish colony of Connecticut.

1642 French settlement at Montréal.

1644 English establish colony of Rhode Island.

1654 Jewish settlement at New Amsterdam.

1663 Carolinas proclaimed English.

1664 New Amsterdam (New York) captured by British.

1670 Hudson's Bay Company established.

1680 Indians expel Spanish from New Mexico.

1682 Pennsylvania founded by William Penn.

1684 La Salle claims French Louisiana.

1689–92 Spanish recapture New Mexico.

1700 Catholic missions established in Arizona.

1706 Spanish settlement at Albuquerque.

1711–13 War in North Carolina between settlers and Tuscarora Indians.

1714 Britain gains Acadia, Hudson's Bay, and Newfoundland from France under Treaty of Utrecht.

1718 French settlement at New Orleans.

1728 Russian Bering starts exploration of Alaska.

1729 Uprising of Natchez Indians in Louisiana.

1733 British found Georgia.

1731–35 French subdue Natchez.

1739–48 War between French and British; raids on Saratoga, Maine, and Albany. British capture Fort Louisbourg.

1754 British capture Fort Duquesne (Pittsburgh).

1759 British capture Québec and Montréal.

1763 French rule in North America ended by Treaty of Paris. Florida ceded from Spanish to British. British declare land west of Appalachian Mountains preserve of Indians; Ottawa Indians rebel.

1764 French expelled from Illinois, establish St. Louis.

1766 British taxes imposed on American colonies.

1768 Ohio River declared boundary between Iroquois Indians and European settlers under Treaty of Fort Stanwix.

1769 British settlements in Kentucky. Spanish missions in California.

1773 Colonists protest over British customs duty at Boston Tea Party.

1774 Québec Act establishes government of Canada, institutes Catholicism and French culture. War between Lord Dunmore and settlers in Virginia.

1775 Battle of Lexington; start of the American Revolution. Spanish found Tucson, Arizona.

1776 United States' Declaration of Independence. Spanish found San Francisco.

1781 Lord Cornwallis surrenders at Battle of Yorktown.

1782 Massacre of Indians by Ohio settlers.

1783 Britain concedes American independence under Treaty of Paris; Florida and French Louisiana under Spanish rule; mass exodus of British colonists to Canada and West Indies.

1784 Russian settlement on Kodiak Island.

1787 Northwest Ordinance promotes settlers' westward expansion.

1789 Washington becomes the first president of the United States.

1791 Québec divided into Upper and Lower Canada. Vermont joins U.S.

1792 Freed slaves return to Africa, found Sierra Leone. Kentucky becomes a state.

1793 Invention of the cotton gin.

1795 Twelve Indian nations agree boundaries with settlers under Treaty of Greenville.

1796 Tennessee joins U.S.

1797 John Adams becomes U.S. president.

1798 Mississippi joins U.S.

1800 Louisiana ceded by Spain to France.

1801 Thomas Jefferson becomes U.S. president.

1803 U.S. purchases Louisiana from France. Ohio joins U.S.

1806 Cumberland Road constructed westward.

1809 Settlers granted 2.5 million acres of Indian land in Ohio and Indiana. Indian nations start uniting under chief Tecumseh against U.S.

1812 Louisiana joins U.S. Russians build Fort Ross, California.

1812–15 War between U.S. and Britain; Indian nations ally with Britain; Tecumseh killed at battle of Moravian Town. War ends with Treaty of Ghent.

1813 Mexican declaration of independence.

1815 Sioux Indian lands south of Lake Michigan

opened to European settlement by Treaty of Portages.

1816 Clashes between settlers and Méti Indians in Canada. Indiana joins U.S.

1817 Mississippi joins U.S. First Seminole Indian War; Andrew Jackson invades Florida.

1818 Illinois joins U.S. Kickapoo Indians resist expulsion.

1819 U.S. purchases Florida from Spain.

1820 Maine joins U.S. Missouri Compromise between slave and nonslave states.

1821 Alabama and Missouri join the U.S. Mexico wins independence.

1822 Attempted slave rebellion brutally suppressed in Charleston, South Carolina.

1823 The Monroe Doctrine of European/American separation.

1825 John Quincy Adams becomes U.S. president. Erie Canal opened.

1827 Winnebago uprising in Wisconsin.

1829 Andrew Jackson becomes U.S. president.

1830 Indian Removal Act; Indian nations relocated to provide settlers new land.

1833 Slavery abolished throughout British Empire.

1835–37 Toledo War over Ohio-Michigan boundary.

1835–42 Second Seminole Indian War in Florida.

1836 Arkansas joins U.S. Texas wins independence from Mexico.

1837 Michigan joins U.S. Martin Van Buren becomes U.S. president.

1845 U.S. annexes Texas. War between U.S. and Mexico. Florida joins U.S. James Knox Polk becomes U.S. president.

1846 U.S. captures Los Angeles and California. Iowa joins U.S. Britain cedes Oregon to U.S. Canadian border set by Treaty of Oregon.

1847 Mexicans defeated by U.S. at Battle of Buena Vista; U.S. troops occupy Mexico City. Mormon Salt Lake City founded in Utah. Start of major influx of Irish immigrants to the U.S.

1848 U.S. captures territory up to Rio Grande (New Mexico). Wisconsin joins U.S.

1849 California gold rush. Zachary Taylor becomes U.S. president.

1850 California joins U.S. Mariposa War between prospectors and Indians. Clay Compromise restricts slavery. Millard Fillmore becomes U.S. president.

1853 U.S. purchases southern Arizona from Mexico. Franklin Pierce becomes U.S. president.

1854 Northern Indian territories become states of Kansas and Nebraska; pro- and anti-slavery clashes. Great Northern Railway completed in Canada.

1855 Ottawa becomes Canadian capital. Third Seminole Indian War in Florida.

1858 Minnesota joins U.S. Colorado gold rush.

1859 First oil well, in Pennsylvania.

1860 Abraham Lincoln elected president. South Carolina secedes from Union over abolition of slavery. War between settlers and Paiute Indians in Nevada.

1861 Virginia, North Carolina, Arkansas, Tennessee, Alabama, Florida, Texas, Louisiana, Mississippi, and Georgia form a Confederate government of southern slave states. U.S. president Abraham Lincoln unites remaining states in anti-slavery stance. The American Civil War begins with the Confederate siege and capture of Fort Sumter, South Carolina. Clashes in Missouri, Virginia, and along South Atlantic coast. Apache uprisings in Southwest.

1862 Clashes in Kentucky, Tennessee, Arkansas, Mississippi. Sieges of Forts Henry and Donelson. Battle of Shiloh. Campaigns in New Mexico, North Carolina, Shenandoah Valley, Manassas. Battles of Gaines' Mill, Malvern Hill, Antietam, Fredericksburg. Confederate invasion of Kentucky. Battles of Iuka and Corinth. Vicksburg campaigns begin. Indian lands in

Kansas and Nebraska opened to settlers. Sioux uprisings in Minnesota and North Dakota.

1863 Battle of Stones River. Union captures Vicksburg. Siege of Port Hudson. Battle of Chancellorsville. Confederate invasion of Pennsylvania; Confederate campaign to take Gettysburg fails. Battle for Charleston. Tullahoma campaign; Union captures Chattanooga. Battle of Chickamauga. Siege of Chattanooga. Knoxville campaign. Emacipation Proclamation.

1864 Clashes in Mississippi, Florida, Arkansas. The Red River campaign. Battles of Spotsylvania, North Anna, Cold Harbor. Union campaigns against Petersburg and Richmond. Confederate attack on Washington fails. Union's campaign to capture Atlanta at length succeeds. Union captures Mobile Point, Alabama. Clashes in Shenandoah Valley, Missouri, Tennessee. Union victory at battle of Nashville. Nevada joins Union.

1865 Union attacks in Carolinas. Falls of Fort Fisher, Petersburg, and Richmond. Confederates' retreat and final surrender at Appomattox River. Lincoln assassinated. Andrew Johnson becomes president. Slavery abolished throughout U.S.

1866 Railroad Act allows appropriation of Indian lands.

1867 U.S. acquires Alaska from Russia. Dominion of Canada established.

1869 Trans-continental railway completed in U.S.; growth of Chicago. Freed slaves given voting rights. Suppression of Méti uprising in Manitoba. Prince Rupert's Land joins Canada.

1870 Manitoba joins Canada.

1871 British Columbia joins Canada. The Great Fire of Chicago.

1872 Modoc uprisings in Oregon and California.

1874 Gold rush in South Dakota. Indian uprisings in southern plains.

1876 Colorado joins U.S. Sioux, Cheyenne, and Arapaho resistance to westward spread of settlers. Indian lands annexed by Canadian government.

1879 Woolworth opens first store.

1882 U.S. bans Chinese immigration. Alberta, Saskatchewan, and Assiniboia become provinces of Canada.

1885 Suppression of Méti uprising in Saskatchewan. Canadian Pacific railway completed.

1887 General Allotment Act allocates Indian reservations.

1889 Settlers allowed onto Indian lands in Oklahoma. Montana, Washington, and North and South Dakota become states of U.S.

1890 Idaho and Wyoming become states of U.S.

1896 Klondike gold rush in the Yukon, Canada. Utah becomes state of U.S.

1898 Spanish–U.S. war over Cuban independence, and for control of the Caribbean and of the Pacific. U.S. destroys Spanish fleet at Santiago de Cuba, establishes Guantanamo naval base on Cuba, occupies Puerto Rico and the Philippine Islands.

1901 McKinley assassinated; Theodore Roosevelt becomes U.S. president. Creek Indian uprising in Oklahoma.

1903 U.S. takes control of Panama from Colombia. Alaska–British Columbia boundary agreed. First powered flight by the Wright brothers.

1906 Severe earthquake devastates San Francisco.

1912 New Mexico and Arizona become states of U.S.

1913 Woodrow Wilson becomes U.S. president. Henry Ford institutes car production assembly line for Model T. Start of migration of southern blacks to northern cities; growth of Harlem, New York.

1916 U.S. intervenes in Mexican revolution.

1917 Indiscriminate German submarine attacks in

the Atlantic force U.S. to enter World War I.

1918 President Wilson's "Fourteen Points."

1919 Liquor outlawed in U.S.

1920 U.S. women granted voting rights. First public radio broadcasts in U.S.

1921 Immigration restrictions imposed in U.S.

1923 Foundation of General Motors. Massive growth of automobile production in U.S.

1926 Constitutional crisis in Canada. U.S. troops intervene in Nicaragua.

1929 Further immigration restrictions imposed in U.S. Wall Street stock market crash; the Depression.

1931 Drought and dust storms in Canadian prairies spread southward. Completion of Empire State Building, New York.

1933 Franklin D. Roosevelt becomes U.S. president; announces "New Deal." Unemployed put to work on public projects.

1936 Pan-American peace and trade "Reciprocity Treaty." Kodachrome color transparency film marketed.

1939 World War II. Canadian troops stationed in Britain.

1941 Japanese bomb U.S. fleet at Pearl Harbor. U.S. declares war on Central powers.

1942 German U-boat attacks along Eastern U.S. War starts for control of the Pacific. U.S. troops stationed in Britain. U.S. air raids on Tokyo. U.S. forces surrender in Philippines. U.S. Japanese interned. U.S. air raids in Europe. U.S. troops land in Africa. Fermi assembles first nuclear reactor.

1943 U.S. air raids on Germany. Battle of Atlantic reaches height. U.S. submarine war against Japanese. Anglo-American invasion of Italy. U.S. captures Pacific islands.

1944 Allied D-Day landings in Normandy. U.S. advances in Pacific, retakes Philippines.

1945 U.S. invades Okinawa. U.S. drops atomic bombs on Hiroshima and Nagasaki. Japanese surrender. Yalta and Potsdam conferences draw "Iron Curtain" between communist eastern and noncommunist western Europe. The Cold War begins between USA and USSR spheres of influence. United Nations convened. Death of Roosevelt; Harry Truman becomes U.S. president.

1947 Oilfields discovered in Canada.

1948 U.S. Marshall plan for European economic recovery. Invention of the transistor (U.S.).

1949 Newfoundland joins Canada. North Atlantic Treaty Organization (NATO) founded.

1950 Senator Joseph McCarthy's pursuit of U.S. communists begins. UN establishes headquarters in New York. U.S. involvement in Korean War.

1951 First nuclear power station (U.S.).

1952 General Eisenhower becomes U.S. president. Contraceptive pill becomes available.

1954 U.S. schools racially desegregated.

1957 Civil Rights Act in U.S. Integration in schools enforced.

1958 Alaska and Hawaii become 49th and 50th U.S. states. *Explorer 1*, first U.S. satellite, launched.

1959 Opening of St. Lawrence Seaway. Communist Fidel Castro wins power in Cuba.

1960 John F. Kennedy elected U.S. president.

1961 First U.S. advisers sent to Vietnam. Abortive Bay of Pigs U.S. invasion of Cuba.

1962 Cuban missile crisis; Russians back down.

1963 Battle of Ap Bac; serious U.S. involvement in Vietnam. Kennedy assassinated; Lyndon Johnson becomes U.S. president.

1964 First U.S. space probes *Ranger 6* and 7 reach the moon.

1965 Civil rights marches in U.S.; race riots in Los Angeles. Further escalation of U.S. involvement in Vietnam War.

1966 Race riots spread to many U.S. cities.

1967 Canada's 100th anniversary. French President De Gaulle's "Free Québec" speech in Canada. Lyndon Johnson proposes Vietnam peace plan.

1968 Liberal Party under Pierre Trudeau wins election in Canada; Québec separatist movement grows. Assassinations in U.S. of Martin Luther King, Jr., and Robert Kennedy; Republican Richard Nixon elected U.S. president.

1969 U.S. astronaut Neil Armstrong the first man on the moon. Height of the "flower power" movement; Woodstock rock music festival; the shooting at Altamont; the Manson killings.

1970 Students killed at Kent State University anti-Vietnam War protest.

1971 Nixon introduces détente with USSR and China.

1972 Nixon visits China and Russia. SALT I arms limitation treaty signed by U.S. and USSR. U.S. Democratic Party campaign offices burglarized. Nixon reelected.

1973 Completion of World Trade Center, New York.

1974 Watergate investigation (U.S.); Nixon admits cover-up, resigns. French becomes official language of Québec.

1975 Fall of Saigon; U.S. withdrawal from Vietnam. Olympic games held in Montréal.

1976 Democrat Jimmy Carter elected U.S. president.

1978 Peace accord between Egypt and Israel signed at Camp David.

1979 SALT II arms limitation treaty between U.S. and USSR, but not formally ratified. Accident at Three Mile Island nuclear reactor. 63 hostages taken by Iranian students at U.S. embassy in Tehran.

1980 Rescue mission of U.S. embassy in Tehran fails. Québec separatism rejected by referendum; Trudeau reelected in Canada. Republican Ronald Reagan elected U.S. president.

1981 U.S. hostages in Tehran released.

1983 Announcement of U.S. Strategic Defense ("Star Wars") Initiative. Beginning of Strategic Arms Reduction Talks (START) between U.S. and USSR. U.S. invades Grenada.

1984 Conservatives under Brian Mulroney win election in Canada. Reagan reelected U.S. president.

1987 Intermediate-range arms limitation treaty signed by U.S. and USSR.

1988 Republican George Bush becomes U.S. president.

1989 U.S. invades Panama, ousts Manuel Noriega.

1990 Iraq's Saddam Hussein invades Kuwait and threatens Saudi Arabian oilfields.

1991 U.S. leads UN "Desert Storm" mission to recapture Kuwait. Iraq driven back; Saddam Hussein's regime survives. Dissolution of USSR and Warsaw Pact. START arms reduction treaty signed by U.S. and Russian Federation.

1992 Democrat Bill Clinton elected U.S. president.

1993 North American Free Trade Agreement signed (NAFTA) between U.S., Canada, and Mexico. U.S. bombing of Iraqi military sites. Abortive U.S./UN peacekeeping mission to Somalia. Siege by FBI at Waco, Texas, of the Branch Davidian sect. Bombing of World Trade Center; Islamic extremists suspected.

1994 U.S. intervenes in Haiti, restores President Aristide. Peasant uprising in Chiapas, Mexico.

1996 Olympic games held in Atlanta. Bombing of Oklahoma federal administration building; growth of rural, extreme right-wing groups.

Select Bibliography

The authors readily acknowledge the work of many scholars and publications that have been consulted in the preparation of this atlas. Following is a selected bibliography of works recommended for further reading on the topics covered in this atlas.

Asante, M. K. and M. T. Mattson, *Historical and Cultural Atlas of African Americans*, Macmillan, 1992.

Bailyn, Bernard, *Voyagers to the West: A Passage in the Peopling of America on the Eve of the Revolution*, New York, 1986.

Beck, W. A. and Y. D. Haase, *Historical Atlas of the American West*, University of Oklahoma Press, 1989.

Bell, C., *The Diplomacy of Détente: The Kissinger Era*, New York, 1977.

Bledsoe, A. J., *The Indian Wars of the Northwest*, San Francisco, 1885.

Blum, J. M., *Years of Discord: American Politics and Society, 1961–1974*, Norton, 1991.

Boatner, Mark, *The Civil War Dictionary, 2nd. Ed.*, 1991

Brogan, H., *The Pelican History of the United States of America*, Penguin Books, 1986.

Brotherstone, G., *Images of the New World*, Thames & Hudson, 1979.

Brown, Wallace, and Hereward Senior, *Victorious in Defeat: The Loyalists in Canada*, New York, 1984.

Bumstead, H. M., *The Peoples of Canada*, Oxford University Press, 1992.

Carnes, Mark C., Editor, *Mapping Americas Past*, Henry Holt & Company, 1997

Catlin, George, *North American Indians*, Leary, Stuart & Co., 1920.

Coe, M. D., *The Maya*, Thames & Hudson, 1966.

Coe, Michael, Dean Snow, and Elizabeth Benson, *Atlas of Ancient America*, Facts on File, 1986.

Conrad, M., A. Finkel, and C. Jaenen, *History of the Canadian Peoples, vol. 1 Beginnings to 1867; vol. 2 1867 to the Present*, Copp, Clark, Pitman, 1993.

Crockatt, R., *The Fifty Years War: The United States and the Soviet Union in World Politics, 1941–1991*, Routledge, 1995.

Crosby, A. E., Jr., *The Columbian Exchange*, Greenwood, 1972.

Cumming, W. P., R. A. Skelton, and D. B. Quinn, *The Discovery of North America*, London, 1971.

Cumming, W. P., S. E. Hillier, D. B. Quinn, and Glyndwr

Williams, *The Exploration of North America 1630-1776*, London, 1974.

Daniels, Roger, *Coming to America. A History of Immigration and Ethnicity in American Life*, New York, 1990.

Davies, N., *The Aztecs*, University of Oklahoma Press, 1980.

DeVoto, Bernard, *The Course of Empire*, Boston, 1952.

Dixon, E. James, *Quest for the Origins of the First Americans*, University of New Mexico Press, 1993

Droyson, G., ed., *Allgemeiner Historischer Handatlas*, Velhagen & Klasing, 1886.

Duffy, S., Editor, *The Macmillan Atlas of Irish History*, Macmillan, 1997.

Dulles, F. R., *America's Rise to World Power 1891–1954*, Harper & Row, 1955.

Eccles, W. J., *Essays on New France*, Oxford University Press, 1987.

Fagan, Brian M., *Ancient North America: The Archaeology of a continent*, (2nd edition), Thames & Hudson, New York, 1985.

Fagan, Brian M., *The Great Journey: The Peopling of Ancient America*, Thames & Hudson, 1987.

Ferrell, R. H. and R. Natkiel, *Atlas of American History*, Facts On File, 1987.

Fladmark, Knut R., *Routes: Alternative migration corridors for Early Man in North America*. American Antiquity 44, 1979, pp. 55–69.

Foote, Shelby, *The Civil War: A Narrative*, 3 vols., Random House, 1958–1974.

Fox, Edward W. ed., *Atlas of American History*, Oxford University Press, 1964.

Garthoff, R. L., *Détente and Confrontation: American-Soviet Relations from Nixon to Reagan*, Washington D. C., 1985.

Gerlach, Arch C., ed., *The National Atlas of the United States of America*, Washington, D. C., 1970.

Gibson, C., *Spain in America*, Harper & Row, 1967.

Gilbert, Martin, *Atlas of American History* (2nd rev. ed.), Dorset Press, 1985.

Glazer, N. and Moynahan, D. P., *Beyond the Melting Pot*, Massachusetts Institute of Technology Press, 1963.

Graebner, N. A., *America as a World Power*, Wilmington, Delaware, 1984.

Hagan, W. T., *American Indians*, University of Chicago Press, 1961.

Harrington, M., *The Other America*, Penguin Books.

Harris R. Cole, et al., eds., 3 vols., *Historical Atlas of Canada*, University of Toronto Press, 1987–1993.

Hoerder, Dirk, ed., *American Labor and Immigration History, 1877–1920s: Recent European Research*, 1983.

Hofstadter, R., *The Age of Reform from Bryan to F. D. R.*, Alfred A. Knopf, 1955.

Homberger, Eric, *The Historical Atlas of New York City*, Henry Holt and Co., 1994.

Jackson, Kenneth T., ed. (2nd ed.), *Atlas of American*

History, Scribner's Sons, 1978.

Jennings, Jesse D., *Prehistory of North America*, 3rd ed., Mayfield Pub. Co., 1989.

Karnow, Stanley, *Vietnam: A History*, New York, Viking Press 1983

Kennedy, Paul, *The Rise and Fall of the Great Powers*, Unwin-Hyman, 1987.

Knight, A., *The Mexican Revolution*, 2 vols., Cambridge University Press, 1986.

Macpherson, James M., *The Atlas of the Civil War*, Macmillan, 1994.

Meinig, D. W., *The Shaping of America, vol. 1 Atlantic America 1492–1800, vol. 2 Continental America 1800–1867*, Yale University Press, 1986, 1993.

Meyer, M. C., and W. I. Sherman, *The Course of Mexican History*, Oxford University Press, 1991.

Middleton, Richard, *Colonial America, a History, 1585–1776*, (2nd edition), Blackwell, Oxford, 1996.

Miller, R. R., *Mexico: A History*, University of Oklahoma Press, 1985.

Miller, Theodore R., *Graphic History of the Americas*, John Wiley & Sons, 1969.

Mitchel, R. D. and P. A. Groves, eds., *North America: The Historical Georgraphy of a Changing Continent*, Hutchinson, 1987.

Morris, R. B., *Encyclopedia of American History*, rev. ed., Harper & Row, 1965.

Morison, S. E., *The Oxford History of the American People*, Oxford University Press, 1965.

Morison, S. E., *The European Discovery of America: The Northern Voyages*, New York, 1971.

Nugent, Walter, *Crossings. The Great Transatlantic Migrations, 1870–1914*, Bloomington, Ind., 1992.

Oxford Regional Economic Atlas. The United States and Canada (2nd ed.), Oxford University Press, 1975.

Paullin, Charles O., *Atlas of the Historical Geography of the United States*, Carnegie Institution, American Geographical Society of New York, 1932.

Portinario, P., and F. Knirsch, *The Cartography of North America 1500–1800*, New York, 1987.

Quinn, D. B., *North America from the Norse Voyages to 1612*, Harper & Row, 1977.

Rawley, J. A., *The Transatlantic Slave Trade*, Norton, 1981.

Rodman, Paul, *Mining Frontiers of the Far West, 1848–1880*, New York, 1963.

Rooney John F., et al., *This Remarkable Continent: An Atlas of United States and Canadian Society and Cultures*, Texas A & M University Press, 1982.

Ruggles, Richard I., *A Country so Interesting: The Hudson's Bay Company and Two Centuries of Mapping 1670–1870*, 1991.

Singletary, O., *The Mexican War*, University of Chicago Press, 1960.

Stampp, K. M., *The Peculiar Institution: Slavery in the Ante Bellum South*, Alfred A. Knopf, 1956.

Stilgoe, J., *Metropolitan Corridor: Railroads and the American Scene*, Yale University Press, 1983.

Summers, H. G. Jr., *Historical Atlas of the Vietnam War* Hougton Mifflin Company, 1995.

Summers, H. G. Jr., *The New World Strategy: A Military Policy for America's Future*, Simon and Schuster/Touchstone Books, 1995.

Taylor Henry L., *Race and the City: Work, Community and Protest in Cincinnati, 1820–1970*, ed. Henry Louis Taylor, Jr., University of Illinois Press, 1993.

Weber, David J. *The Spanish Frontier in North America*, Yale University Press, 1992.

Wiebe, R. H., *The Search for Order 1877–1920*, Macmillan, 1967.

Winzerlins, Oscar W., *Acadian, Odyssey*, Baton Rouge, 1955.

Wood, G. S., *The Creation of the American Republic, 1776–1787*, Norton, 1972.

Zuckerman, S., *Nuclear Illusion and Reality*, London, 1982.

INDEX

Acknowledgments

Pictures are reproduced by permission of, or have been provided by the following:

Corbis: pp. 132, 135
Culver Pictures: 138
e.t. archive: pp. 12, 18, 22, 116, 118
Historical Society of Pennsylvania: p. 36
Hulton Getty: pp. 65, 76, 82, 84, 85, 96, 98, 101, 102, 107, 114, 122, 123, 127
Image Bank: pp. 44, 125, 140, 149
Library of Congress: pp. 63, 79
National Archives: pp. 60, 68, 93, 112
New York Historical Society: p. 39
Peter Newark Historical Pictures: pp. 49, 74, 80, 108
Private Collections: pp. 20, 46, 53, 90, 101, 130
U.S. Army Military Historical Institute: p. 62
Utah State Historical Society: p. 58
Werner Forman Archive: pp. 10, 14, 16, 34, 87
Yale University Art Gallery: p. 32

Design: Malcolm Swanston

Typesetting: Shirley Ellis

Cartography: Peter Gamble, Elsa Gibert, Malcolm Swanston, Isabelle Verpaux, Jonathan Young

Production: Marion M. Storz

DATE DUE

4/08			
GAYLORD			PRINTED IN U.S.A.